Technology
and American
Economic Growth

TECHNOLOGY AND AMERICAN ECONOMIC GROWTH

Nathan Rosenberg

M. E. SHARPE, INC., ARMONK, NEW YORK

Library of Congress Catalog Card Number: 76-52621
International Standard Book Number: 0-87332-104-9

In Memory
of Michael Wollan
1943–1968

Contents

Preface

This book represents an attempt to explore the relationship between technological change and the long-term economic growth of the American economy. It is hoped that it will provide the conceptual framework, the basic facts and the historical perspective which are essential to a better understanding of a highly important subject. It hardly needs to be said that such a small book cannot possibly treat such a big subject in an authoritative way. But the fundamental difficulty is not really one of space; rather, it is our still limited and imperfect understanding of the causes and consequences of the immensely complicated social process which we call technological change. Moreover, we continue to be woefully uninformed concerning important portions of our historical past. We retain misconceptions and misinformation about this past which inhibit a better understanding of the subject of this book. As that wise man, Mark Twain, once observed, the trouble with the world isn't ignorance—it's people knowing all them things that ain't so. One of the objects of this book will therefore be to establish a clearer line of demarcation between the realms of historical fact and fancy. Its main purpose, however, is to provide an interpretive framework within which we can enlarge our understanding of the manner in which technology has shaped the development of the American economy and, as a result, American society more generally.

This book first began to take shape during the academic year 1968–69, when I was a Research Associate at the Harvard University Program on Technology and Society. The writing began in earnest when I joined the Economics Department of the University of Wisconsin in the fall of 1969, and was completed during the spring of 1970 while I was a visitor at Nuffield College, Oxford, and in the latter part of 1970 when I was a visiting professor in the Department of Economics at the University of the Philippines under the auspices of the Rockefeller Foundation. To each of these institutions I am deeply grateful.

I count myself as one who has been exceedingly well-endowed with friends and colleagues who have given generously of their time and counsel. My greatest debts—and they are debts of long standing—are to Richard A. Easterlin, William N. Parker, and Eugene Smolensky. I have learned much from this formidable trio. If I have not learned even more, the fault is surely mine alone. I have particularly benefited also from comments and suggestions from Stanley Engerman, Peter Mathias, Vernon Ruttan, and Nicholas von Tunzelmann.

An earlier, much shorter version of the present volume appears as Chapter VII in Lance Davis et al., *American Economic Growth*, Harper and Row, New York, 1971. I am grateful to Harper and Row, and most especially to John Greenman, for the encouragement which led to the expansion of that chapter into the present book.

A slightly modified version of Chapter III was presented at a symposium on the transfer of industrial technology in the nineteenth century which was sponsored by the International Cooperation in the History of Technology Committee at Pont-à-Mousson, France, in July 1970. Chapter IV draws, in a few places, upon two of my earlier works, "Technological Change in the Machine Tool Industry, 1840–1910," *Journal of Economic History*, December 1963, and the Editor's Introduction to *The American System of Manufactures*, Edinburgh University Press, Edinburgh, 1969. The final chapter draws slightly upon a paper delivered in Aspen, Colorado in September 1970 at a conference on the subject: "Technology: Social Goals and Cultural Options." The conference was sponsored by the International Association for Cultural Freedom and the Aspen Institute for Humanistic Studies. That paper was published in *Technology and Culture*, October 1971, under the title: "Technology and the Environment: An Economic Exploration."

Michael Wollan, to whom this book is dedicated, was a young lawyer of great promise who had just begun to contribute to the study of the legal and social problems of technological change when his life was tragically cut short by an automobile accident. He was also a friend of rare personal charm. He is sorely missed.

Madison, Wisconsin

CHAPTER I

Technology in Historical Perspective

GENERAL CONSIDERATIONS

It is possible, and illuminating as a first approximation, to consider technological progress as any improvement in the relationship between inputs and outputs. That is, if we conceive of an economic system as a single gigantic factory (or farm), we may say that technological progress consists of those improvements in methods of production which make it possible to achieve more output with the same volume of resources, or the same output with a smaller volume of resources. In somewhat more technical jargon, such a change represents a shift in the production function. It is important that such shifts be distinguished from other ways of increasing the output of an economic system. To cite the most obvious alternative, an economy (or factory or farm) could increase its output simply by using more inputs. People may work longer hours, or a larger proportion of the population may enter the labor force, or a larger proportion of incomes may be saved and used to accumulate more capital.[1] In fact, a serious understanding of the process by which economic growth takes place would require that we sort out the relative importance of these separate sources of growth. This is much easier to do conceptually than it is empirically, partly because many new techniques must be embodied in new kinds of capital equipment and skills before they can become economically significant. Moreover, some of the most interesting and subtle aspects of the process of economic change concern the *interrelationships* among the various sources of such change, the dependence of the behavior of one variable upon the simultaneous behavior of one or more other variables.

Nevertheless, we may begin by assuming that, at a given moment in time, there exists a spectrum of known ways in which resources may be combined to produce a given volume of final output. Which of these technically feasible combinations will be selected—which one will minimize costs—will depend upon the prices, and therefore upon the available supplies, of the various resource inputs. The optimum input combination will change as input prices change (Figure 1). Thus, if the supply of capital should be increasing more rapidly than the supply of labor and if, as a result, labor is becoming relatively more expensive than capital, we would expect this to lead to a shift to more capital-intensive methods—A_1 to A_2 to A_3.

On the other hand, the optimum input combination will also change as a result of the introduction of a new and superior technique. In Figure 2 this is represented by an inward shift of

1. A further possibility is that there may be economies of large-scale production. Where such economies exist, a given percentage increase in inputs will result in a greater percentage increase in output. This is the essential explanation for the distinctive concentration of manufacturing activity, in industrial economies, in factories employing large amounts of capital and labor within the confines of a single establishment and producing a volume of output far beyond the requirements of local consumption.

the isoquant from 1 to 2—i.e., it becomes possible to produce the same volume of output with a smaller volume of inputs than previously. This case, in contrast to the first one, represents an improvement in total resource productivity and its pervasive importance in the long run is a main reason for our interest in the role of technological change in the growth of the American economy.

In examining the historical role of technological change, it would be a highly instructive exercise to visualize the American economy in the year 1800—an economy which was overwhelmingly agricultural, employing relatively little capital, with production mostly for local markets and with only the most rudimentary forms of land transportation, with low population densities, and with productive activity typically centered upon the family unit. Let us assume, for such an economy, a total absence of all changes in techniques. What would this economy look like if there were no natural resource constraints upon its growth, if it could grow by adding to its stock of capital more and more of the tools, equipment, and transport forms vintage 1800, if its population and labor force continued to grow, and if it gradually expanded extensively to exploit the resources of the American continent? The social system conjured up by these suppositions would doubtless have been highly gratifying to Thomas Jefferson, with his vision of a broadly based, egalitarian economy of prosperous, small-holding farmers. But with none of the major improvements in productivity borne by technological change, the late-twentieth-century American economy would be completely inconceivable as a product of this kind of growth.

Our exercise could usefully be carried one step further by dropping our assumption of unlimited resources. After all, it is a matter of simple arithmetic that population growth within

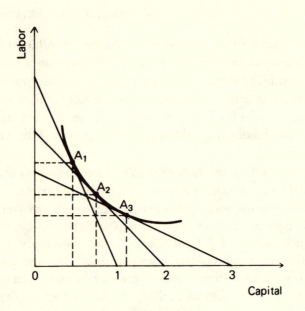

Figure 1

Figure 2

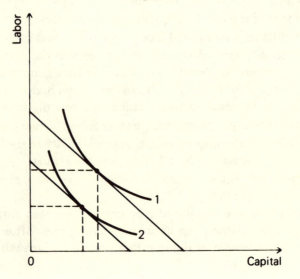

any finite land area means a continued reduction in resources per capita. It seems plausible to argue that eventually this reduction in resource inputs per capita will impose serious constraints upon the society's capacity to increase its output per capita. Let us continue to assume that we are dealing with the prospects for economic growth in a society experiencing little or no technological progress, but where in addition the supply of unutilized land has been essentially exhausted. (Frederick Jackson Turner's well-known "frontier thesis," first presented in 1893, takes the year 1890 as marking the close of the American frontier. Nevertheless, the land area under cultivation in the United States continued to grow at a rapid rate until 1920.) Such a society can continue to make additions to its (qualitatively unchanged) capital stock, but if the available land is already being intensively cultivated, and if, furthermore, population is continuing to grow at a rapid pace, then the prospects for the future are indeed dim.

We have, in fact, sketched out the essential features of a Malthusian-Ricardian world.[2] It was precisely in considering the future prospects for such a society that the classical economists first discovered and examined the historical implications of the law of diminishing returns. Their dreary prognostications were the product of their reflections over the long-run prospects for a society experiencing (1) an unalterable land constraint, (2) continuing population growth, and therefore (3) a declining rate of growth of total output. Within the framework of their reasoning, a stationary state, characterized by low or zero profits, no capital accumulation, and a maximum attainable population size barely surviving at subsistence-level in-

2. Notice that the first edition of Malthus's famous essay, published (anonymously) in 1798, bore the complete title: "Essay on the Principle of Population as it effects the future improvement of Society, with remarks on the Speculations of Mr. Godwin, M. Condorcet and Others."

comes, seemed alarmingly probable and not very far distant.

If we compare the world of the 1970s with (1) the world of the 1800s and (2) the dreary conclusions of the futurologists of that generation, it is clear that, in the industrialized countries at least, a major reason for the differences lies in the complete failure to anticipate the improvements in productivity which have resulted from technological change.[3] Economists in the past decade or so have been busily at work attempting to repair this past neglect. When they addressed themselves to the question posed earlier, of the relative importance to economic growth of using more inputs versus using inputs more efficiently, it turned out that the latter source seemed to be overwhelmingly the most important. The first quantitative studies for the United States suggested that no more than 15 percent or so of the observed rise in per capita incomes could be accounted for by growth in the (qualitatively unchanged) stock of capital per worker.[4] These studies were, methodologically

3. There is an interesting point here in the almost congenital pessimism of professional judgments on the possibilities for technological change over the years. Simon Kuznets has made the following observations on the subject: "Experts are usually specialists skilled in, and hence bound to, traditional views; and they are, because of their knowledge of one field, likely to be cautious and unduly conservative. Hertz, a great physicist, denied the practical importance of shortwaves, and others at the end of the 19th century reached the conclusion that little more could be done on the structure of matter. Malthus, Ricardo, and Marx, great economists, made incorrect prognoses of technological changes at the very time that the scientific bases for these changes were evolving. On the other hand, imaginative tyros like Jules Verne and H. G. Wells seemed to sense the potentialities of technological change. It is well to take cognizance of this consistently conservative bias of experts in evaluating the hypothesis of an unlimited effective increase in the stock of knowledge and in the corresponding potential of economic growth" Simon Kuznets, *Economic Growth and Structure* (New York: W. W. Norton, 1965), p. 89.

4. The pioneering articles were Moses Abramovitz, "Resource and Output Trends in the United States since 1870," *American Economic Review, Papers and Proceedings*, May 1956, pp. 5–23 and Robert Solow, "Technical Change and the Aggregate Production Function," *Review of Economics and Statistics*, August 1957, pp. 312–320.

speaking, very crude, and a good deal of effort is being devoted to developing more refined measures of the role of a range of factors which contribute to economic growth. Whatever the eventual refinements in these estimates, it now seems clearly established that technological change has made a massive contribution to the growth of the American economy.

The relative importance of technological change as a contributor to the long-term rise in productivity of the economy will depend, of course, partly on how broadly or narrowly it is defined. If one defines technological change in the broadest possible sense to encompass all changes in knowledge which contribute to the productivity of resources (as have some writers in the past), then of course technological change becomes virtually coterminous with productivity growth. If, on the other hand, one restricts the meaning of technological change to a narrower, "hardware" definition (of a kind recognized by the U.S. Patent Office) then its contribution is severely restricted. Furthermore, whatever the contribution of technological change to productivity growth, it is a serious mistake to believe that these changes have always been dependent upon *recent* increments to the stock of knowledge, although it may well be true that this dependence has been increasing in recent years. As Denison has forcefully asserted:

The advance of productivity is sometimes discussed as if it were very largely the result of new technological knowledge. But surely this is wrong. Dramatic advances in management and organizational techniques and in architectural layout are visible to the naked eye. It would be difficult to find technological innovations with an impact on production exceeding that of the introduction of interchangeable parts, or of the assembly line, or of time and motion study and all that has flowed from it. Managerial and organizational advances have recently slashed the requirement for holding inventories. The design of factory build-ings has been radically changed to permit the easy flow of materials, and that of office buildings to provide more usable space. Improve-ments in work scheduling, in personnel management and labor rela-tions, and in methods of appraising and reaching potential markets are in this category, as are the whole fields of business organization and the management structure of business enterprises and other producing organizations.[5]

The productivity-increasing impact of technological change has had major effects on the structure and organization of our modern economic system. Many of the differences in the American economies of 1800 and 1970 are ultimately attribut-able to the increasing reliance upon a technology possessing certain kinds of characteristics, and requiring that economic activity be organized in very specific ways. Furthermore, the rapid rate of growth of per capita incomes, which is the most important social end product of improvements in technology, has generated a whole vast chain reaction of consequences be-cause of the different ways in which people at higher levels of income choose to dispose of their incomes.[6] Thus, higher levels

5. Edward F. Denison, *The Sources of Economic Growth in the United States and the Alternatives before Us*, Supplementary Paper No. 13 (New York: Com-mittee for Economic Development, 1962), p. 232. Denison's emphasis on the importance of "software" is an important corrective to a widespread tendency to think of technological change in purely "hardware" terms. Such major inno-vations as the supermarket and the cafeteria were hardly dependent upon significant additions to our stock of gadgets or machinery. Rather, they may be thought of as productivity-increasing innovations which were made possible by a drastic modification of the manner in which certain services are provided. In addition therefore, and no less important, these innovations involved a willing-ness on the part of the consumer to accept a *different* service, one in which he in fact participates in a more active way by substituting his own labor for that of a clerk or waitress.
6. For the 120-year period from 1840 to 1960 the population of the United States grew at an average rate of about 2% per year; GNP at 3.6% per year; and product per capita at 1.6% per year. Per capita GNP for 1840, expressed in 1961 dollars, is placed at $446, as compared to $2829 for 1959–61.

of per capita income have been associated with changes in the composition of aggregate demand and therefore final output. Perhaps the most spectacular and far-reaching is the decline in the relative importance of the agricultural sector, as the percentage of consumer expenditures on food products declines. The rise in the relative importance of the manufacturing sector is well known. Less attention, however, has been paid to the growth of that complex of activities rather indiscriminately lumped together into a heterogeneous collection called "the services sector."[7] The impact of technology underlies not only the changing productivity of our economic inputs, but also the drastic changes in the composition of output and the shifting composition and allocation of inputs. This is readily apparent in changes in the industrial composition of the labor force. Industrial technologies exhibit strong tendencies toward the geo-

	Annual U.S. Growth Rates (Percent)		
Period	Product	Population	Product per Capita
1840–1880	4.03	2.73	1.26
1880–1920	3.52	1.88	1.61
1920–1960	3.15	1.31	1.81
1840–1960	3.56	1.97	1.56

Simon Kuznets, "Notes on the Pattern of U.S. Economic Growth," in Edgar O. Edwards (ed.), *The Nation's Economic Objectives* (Chicago: University of Chicago Press, 1964), p. 16. Cf. Simon Kuznets, *Modern Economic Growth*, (New Haven, Conn.: Yale University Press, 1966), chap. 2.

7. "The services sector comprises a variety of economic activities, ranging from professional pursuits demanding high skill and large investment in training to domestic service and other unskilled personal services; from activities with large capital investment, such as residential housing, to those requiring no material capital; from pursuits closely connected with the private market, such as trade, banking and related financial and business services, to government activities, including defense, in which market considerations are limited. They have one basic feature in common: none of the activities represents in any significant way the production of commodities; each renders a product that is intangible and not easily embodied in a lasting and measurable form. . . . " Kuznets, *Modern Economic Growth, op. cit.,* pp. 143–144.

graphic concentration of productive activity. Technological indivisibilities which dictate very large producing units far in excess of local requirements, heavy reliance upon the utilization of fossil fuels (themselves highly concentrated geographically) as energy sources, regional specialization of a highly productive agricultural sector: these factors create a powerful trend toward geographic concentration. Since sizable population centers hold out to business firms the additional attractions of large markets for their product as well as specialized services which are not available in smaller communities, the trend toward a high degree of spatial concentration is further reinforced. An inevitable result of such concentration is that an increasing proportion of the economy's resources must necessarily be devoted to transporting and distributing goods to their ultimate points of consumption. Such technological considerations go far toward explaining the increasing commitment of labor to transportation, retailing, sales and distribution generally, storage, credit, and finance. A modern economy cannot function effectively without devoting a substantial portion of its labor force to the ancillary activities made necessary by the unique requirements of an industrial technology.[8]

8. Kuznets, *Modern Economic Growth, op. cit.*, chap. 3. See also the excellent short statement in the article by Richard A. Easterlin, "Economic Growth: Overview," in the *International Encyclopedia of the Social Sciences* (New York: The Macmillan Company and The Free Press, 1968). In a very real sense, the long-term downward decline in the length of the work week and the corresponding importance of leisure-time activities have been the joint product of growing productivity combined with a set of tastes which has treated leisure time as a superior good. But although the long-term downward decline in the length of the work week has been unmistakable, the evidence of the last 25 years or so does not point unambiguously in the direction of a continuation of this trend. It is not at all clear to what extent shorter hours of employment currently reflects worker preferences (as compared to union bargaining tactics, which have frequently taken the form of demanding the same weekly wage for a shorter work week). The growing prevalence of "moonlighting" and the evident widespread willingness to work overtime, even at standard hourly rates, suggests that many people would prefer longer hours and higher money

It should be clear, then, that we can advance very considerably our understanding of the relationship between technological change and the long-term economic growth of the American economy merely by concentrating upon the productivity-increasing aspects of such changes. But this is far from the total story. American society in the 1970s is so vastly different from the world of 1800 not just because technological change makes it possible to produce more output per unit of input but because it has also provided an expanded array of new commodities and services which were undreamed of in 1800. (It is worth noting, however, that although technological change has brought great improvements in agricultural *productivity*, it has yielded relatively little in the way of new agricultural *products*.) It is certainly arguable that our lives have been more profoundly transformed by the new goods and services provided by a dynamic technology than by an increased capacity to produce the limited range of goods and services which existed during the presidency of Thomas Jefferson: by instant communication, high-speed travel, by the world of modern electronics, chemistry, synthetic materials, the medical technologies of birth prevention and death postponement, and the presence of a potentially apocalyptic military capacity. We cannot, then, hope to arrive at a mature understanding of the long-term impact of the process of technological change with-

incomes. All this, plus the substantial increase in female participation in the labor force, even among women from comfortable, middle-income households, strongly suggests that we are still far from having completely internalized the values of a leisure-time-oriented society. Perhaps additionally we are already approaching the plateau beyond which leisure time begins to become an "inferior good"—a likelihood which may be increased by the high money cost attached to many leisure-time activities, such as foreign travel. Perhaps also we are approaching the state delineated in *Henry IV:* "If all the year were playing holidays, to sport would be as tedious as to work."

out recognizing explicitly its effect on the changing composition as well as the volume of the economy's final output.

Consider how technology has altered the activities involved in operating an ordinary American household.[9] The protracted drudgery of food preparation has been substantially reduced by a long series of innovations which have located food preparation and processing in commercial firms and have permitted households to store such goods for prolonged periods of time. These techniques also made possible—the recent evidence of TV dinners to the contrary notwithstanding—the consumption of a much more interesting, variegated, and nutritious range of foods. Canning techniques, which originated in military requirements during the Napoleonic wars, became widespread in the United States in the 1840s and after. Similarly the rise of meat-packing firms and commercial bakeries on the one hand, and the development of an efficient ice box and, later, refrigerators[10] and freezers on the other, sharply compressed the time devoted to food processing and preparation within the household. The sewing machine, which made its commercial appearance in the 1850s, was rapidly introduced into homes in subsequent decades, and drastically reduced the time consumed in making clothing for family members, especially children. American manufacturers sold 1,500,000 sewing machines between 1856 and 1869 and 4,800,000 from 1869 to 1878. The other basic chores of the housewife have been alleviated, after the home became served by electricity, by an impressive collec-

9. For a fascinating examination of the impact of mechanization upon the household, see Siegfried Giedion, *Mechanization Takes Command* (New York: Oxford University Press, 1948), especially Part VI: "Mechanization Encounters the Household."
10. The development of the refrigerated railroad car had been instrumental in delivering the meat from meat-packing plants to households.

tion of household appliances: notably, the vacuum cleaner, water heater, washing machine and drier, and dishwasher.[11] Cooking has been much simplified by the electric and gas stoves but it should also be remembered that the cast-iron kitchen stove, which these typically replaced, was one of the most important domestic innovations in the first half of the nineteenth century. In the heating of homes, wood fires were replaced by coal and later oil and gas were introduced into the central heating unit. When these units were subjected to thermostatic control the heating of homes became completely automated.[12]

The sources of lighting in the American household have passed through a series of improvements from candles and oil lamps in the early nineteenth century to the predominance of kerosene lamps after 1860 and some use of gas lighting in the 1890s and after. All this was swept away by electric lighting in the early decades of the twentieth century—a transition which was much accelerated by the establishment of the Rural Electrification Commission in the 1930s, which subsidized the extension of electrification into rural America.

Another collection of inventions placed the individual household in touch with the outside world and exposed the family to a series of outside ties and influences which have had far-reaching social and cultural consequences. The telephone,

11. For many of the devices essential to the running of a modern, highly capital-intensive American household, what was required was not only electricity but the design and production of a cheap, durable electric motor.

12. It is perhaps worthwhile adding that the diffusion of some of these innovations took place only slowly, and are by no means universally distributed, even today, among American households. Indeed, as late as 1940, more than 20% of all dwelling units which possessed some form of heating equipment were still burning wood. Ten years later about 10% of all such dwelling units (4.3 million) still relied upon wood. Sam Schurr and Bruce C. Netschert, *Energy in the American Economy, 1850–1975* (Baltimore, Md.: The Johns Hopkins Press, 1960) p. 57.

patented in 1876, made possible instantaneous communication with other telephone subscribers. The phonograph, developed in the last quarter of the nineteenth century, brought durable recordings of music and the human voice into the living room.[13] Commercial radio broadcasting began in the 1920s and commercial television broadcasting began after the Second World War. This "plugging-in" of the household to the outside world brought with it new and pervasive cultural influences and brought about dramatic alterations in the pattern of leisure-time activities.

Members of the household who ventured some distance away from their homes would have required, on land, either horse or some form of horse-drawn transport at the beginning of the nineteenth century. Canals became an important alternative after the opening of the highly successful Erie Canal in 1825. Then, starting in the 1830s the country began to be progressively linked up by a railroad network, moving individuals at previously unheard-of speeds. In the first decade of the twentieth century the automobile, providing its owner with a private form of transportation, began its remarkable growth, and the country's network of surfaced roads expanded in response to the automobile's needs (the automobile had been preceded —and assisted—by the bicycle craze of the 1890s, but this ingenious device was used largely for recreational purposes).

---

13. It is an interesting commentary on the limited vision and social imagination of even the most versatile inventor, that Thomas Edison is said to have thought that the phonograph would be useful principally to record the last wishes of old men on their death beds. Similarly, in the years around the turn of the century when the radio was being developed, it was conceived of as nothing more than a way of supplementing the telephone and telegraph as a form of purely private communication in places where conventional wire communication was impracticable—ships at sea and other geographically inaccessible locations.

Commercial aviation, which was initiated in the 1930s (production of the highly reliable DC–3 was begun in 1935) was held up by the Second World War and experienced a mushrooming growth in the postwar years. With the advent of the jet plane it became possible to span a continent—or an ocean—in less than six hours.

One important consequence of these innovations upon the conduct of the household, and the family in general, which should not go unnoticed is the rise in the female labor force participation rate—especially among married women.[14] Several technological forces, including the increasing effectiveness and wider diffusion of birth control technology, worked in this direction. The transfer of traditional household functions outside the household[15] and the availability of a growing range of appliances reduced the time required for the performance of household tasks. At the same time the availability of the increasingly numerous consumer durables—both those which facilitated the performance of housework and those desired for recreational purposes—created a powerful inducement to en-

14. The white female labor participation rate rose from 12.1% in 1890 to 26.9% in 1940, 31.5% in 1950, and 34.1% in 1960. The nonwhite female labor participation rate was far higher in 1890 (39.5%) but varied only within a narrow range. It was 41.2% in 1960. Stanley Lebergott, *Manpower in Economic Growth* (New York: McGraw-Hill Book Company, 1964), Table A–11.

15. Lebergott provides the salutary reminder that housewives in the nineteenth century engaged in much productive activity inside the household which industrialization eventually placed elsewhere. "... [T]he typical married woman in nineteenth-century America made all the children's clothes (the factory output of children's clothing being trivial prior to 1900) as well as her own; baked the family bread; prepared its soups and preserves (and even the family soap through most of the century); washed clothes for six persons without benefit of anything more than a washboard; dusted, cleaned, and performed a variety of other domestic chores. (In 1830 she even wove most of the cloth for the family's garments as well, since factory production had just gotten under way.)" *Ibid.*, p. 58.

ter the labor force in order to earn the incomes with which to purchase them. Finally, those inventions which lowered the cost of office work—the typewriter, telephone and other new office equipment—increased employment opportunities of a kind which were readily undertaken by females.

Aside from the major new products which we have considered so far, technological change has also been responsible for innumerable product alterations and quality changes, some of which are indistinguishable from product innovation itself. Is the ball point pen "just" a modification of the fountain pen and the modern washer and drier "merely" a modernized version of the old-fashioned wringer washing machine? Perhaps. But the effectiveness of antibiotics in the treatment of infectious diseases certainly suggests strongly that their qualitative improvement over earlier medications should be recognized as a difference in kind—frequently the difference between life and death, as the health statistics amply testify. Until Pasteur's research revealed the role of microbes as a cause of disease, and until Lister's announcement of his discovery of antisepsis in 1867, with the subsequent growth of the science of bacteriology and the development of immunological techniques, medical knowledge simply lacked the capacity for the effective treatment of the many scourges which have beset the human race. (Casanova's eighteenth-century observation in his *Memoirs*, that "More people perish at the hands of doctors than are cured by them," probably held true through most of the nineteenth century as well. Casanova, of course, had some very special— and intractable—medical problems.) Moreover, a whole array of pharmaceutical innovations, from the ubiquitous aspirin to vitamins, to more recent antihistamines, tranquilizers, and contraceptive pills have brought more effective release from pain, disease control, freedom from discomfort and stress, and a degree of control over the reproductive consequences of sexual relations of truly massive significance to the human condition, although most difficult to express in quantitative terms. To the extent that technological change has provided us with an enlarged and qualitatively superior collection of goods and services than we formerly possessed, our conventional measure of economic growth—a rise in per capita national income—*understates* the resulting improvement in economic well-being. But this point, of course, cuts both ways. "Although it is sometimes convenient to specify certain dimensions of performance as 'economic' and others as 'non-economic,' this split is highly arbitrary. The production of automobiles, houses, insecticides and airplanes can be quantified in dollar terms and registered in the market place. The losses which result from ignoring aesthetics in land use, noisy environments, the failure of consumers to understand the hazards of some chemicals, and the lethargy with which society deals with the less pleasant consequences of longer life spans, are less susceptible to quantification, but are equally real. An economic system should be judged by how it affects the lives of its citizens, and not by how well it maximizes money profits or measured output."[16]

A more general point is that technology has generated product changes of all sorts, from discrete changes without closely identifiable antecedents to much more numerous, smaller modifications whose cumulative effects are very large. Thus the American landscape is littered with artifacts of a now obsolete or nearly obsolete technology—not only fountain pens and wringer washing machines but also shaving mugs, milk bottles,

16. Richard R. Nelson, Merton J. Peck, and Edward D. Kalachek, *Technology, Economic Growth and Public Policy* (Washington, D.C.: The Brookings Institution, 1967), p. 147.

78 rpm records, inner tubes, automobile seat covers, trolley cars, soap flakes, carbon paper, mason jars, and newsreels. Each of these once widely-used products has now been largely or entirely superseded.

TECHNOLOGY AND RESOURCE ENDOWMENT

Technological knowledge ought to be understood as the sort of information which improves man's capacity to control and to manipulate the natural environment in the fulfillment of human goals, and to make that environment more responsive to human needs.[17] The intimate relationship between technology and environment becomes apparent as soon as one asks the

17. This definition of technology is in conformity with the classic man vs. natural environment conceptualization which received an early social-philosophical formulation in the work of John Locke, and is essentially the modern view. Talcott Parsons, for example, states that ". . . technology is the socially organized capacity for actively controlling and altering objects of the physical environment in the interest of some human want or need." Talcott Parsons, *Societies* (Englewood Cliffs, N.J.: Prentice-Hall, 1966), p. 15. This view represents a useful and legitimate abstraction and is the one adopted here. It should be understood, however, that the view excludes much of importance to a broader understanding of the social impact of technology. Specifically, a considerable amount of technology has as at least one of its uses the manipulation of people and not inanimate things. Commercial advertising on TV and other communication media is an obvious example. Alternatively, although the Winchester repeating rifle improved man's capacities as a hunter of game, it also brought about important changes in power relationships between human groups, such as the westward-moving American settlers and the Plains Indians. In an earlier period Cortes, whose 600 men were equipped with a mere handful of muskets and small cannon, successfully undertook the conquest of Montezuma and the kingdom of Mexico. To define technology solely in terms of the capacity which it provides for the exploitation of the natural environment, then, is to overlook some of its critical social functions. For an absorbing account of the role of changes in military and maritime technology in European expansion during the fifteenth century and after, see Carlo Cipolla, *Guns, Sails and Empires* (New York: Pantheon Books, 1965).

question: What constitutes a natural resource? The answer is not a simple one, but the safest way to begin such an answer is by saying: "It all depends." If we define resources in terms of mineral deposits or acres of potentially arable land, qualifications spring to mind. The Plains Indian did not cultivate the soil; neither coal, oil, nor bauxite constituted a resource to the Indian population or, for that matter, to the earliest European settlers in North America. It was only when technological knowledge had advanced to a certain point that such mineral deposits became potentially usable for human purposes. Even then, the further economic question turns, in part, upon accessibility and cost of extraction. Improvements in oil drilling technology (as well as changing demand conditions) make it feasible to extract oil today from depths which would have been technically impossible fifty years ago and prohibitively expensive twenty years ago.[18] Similarly, low grade taconite iron ores are being routinely exploited today which would have been ignored earlier in the century when the higher-quality ores of the Mesabi range were available in abundance. Oil shale, known to

18. Improvements in technology, it should be noted, ought to be defined to include also the technology of resource *discovery*. The discovery of new deposits has in fact continually falsified pessimistic predictions (based upon the conservative notion of "proved reserves") of imminent exhaustion of oil reserves. "In 1920, the chief geologist of the U.S. Geological Survey reported that petroleum still in the ground and recoverable by contemporary methods amounted to no more than seven billion barrels. It was highly improbable, he added, that the error in this estimate exceeded 50%. Within five years, and possibly within three, petroleum production in the United States, he thought, would pass its peak, and at the annual production rate of half a billion barrels oil resources would be exhausted in fourteen years, that is, by 1934. In fact, when 1934 came twelve, not seven, billion barrels had been recovered and in addition there were twelve billion barrels of "proved reserves." By the middle 1960s, the five billion barrels that had been produced between the beginning of the industry in 1859 and 1920 were being produced every twenty months. Hans H. Landsberg and Sam H. Schurr, *Energy in the United States* (New York: Random House, 1968), p. 98.

exist in vast quantities—for example, in the Green River formation in Colorado, Utah, and Wyoming—is not yet worth exploiting but might well be brought into production if petroleum product prices rise very much above their present levels. The rich and abundant agricultural resources of the Midwest were of limited economic importance until the development of a canal network beginning in the 1820s with the completion of the Erie Canal, and later a railroad system which made possible the transportation of bulky farm products to eastern urban centers at low cost. Natural resources, in other words, cannot be catalogued in geographic or geological terms alone. The economic usefulness of such resources is subject to continual redefinition as a result of both economic changes and alterations in the stock of technological knowledge. Whether a particular mineral deposit is worth exploiting will depend upon all of the forces influencing the demand for the mineral, on the one hand, and the cost of extracting it, on the other.

These observations are highly relevant to the central interests of this book. We have seen that, from a more abstract point of view, a growth in the stock of technological knowledge may be reduced either to (1) a shift in the production function, i.e., an increase in output obtainable from a given quantity of inputs; or (2) the creation of a new production function, i.e., the introduction of a new product or service. But from the perspective of the economic historian surveying the historical experience of the wealth—and poverty—of nations, the production and use of technological knowledge must be seen against the backdrop of specific societies with different cultural heritages and values, different human capital and intellectual equipment, and confronting an environment with a very specific collection of resources. The emphasis on the specificness of resources is important, because resources establish the particular framework of problems, of constraints, and opportunities, to which technological change is the (occasional) human response. Although we may usefully *conceive* of technological change for analytical purposes and for purposes of quantification in an abstract way as an alteration in the relationship between inputs and outputs, it does not *occur* in the abstract but rather in very specific historical contexts. It occurs, that is, as a successful solution to a particular problem thrown up in a particular resource context. For example, the cutting off of an accustomed source of supply during wartime has often been an important stimulus for the development of new techniques. Thus France's early commercial leadership in the production of synthetic alkalis (utilizing the Leblanc process) was, in large measure, a result of her loss of access to her traditional supplies of Spanish barilla during the Napoleonic wars. The Haber nitrogen fixation process was developed by the Germans during World War I when the British blockade deprived them of their imports of Chilean nitrates. The loss of Malayan natural rubber as a result of Japanese occupation in World War II played a critical role in the rapid emergence of the American synthetic rubber industry. On the other hand, the fact that the British led the world in the development of a coal-using technology was hardly surprising in view of the abundance and easy accessibility of her coal deposits and the growing scarcity of her wood-fuel supplies which increasingly constrained the expansion of her industries in the seventeenth and eighteenth centuries. Indeed, the steam engine itself originated as a pump for solving the problem of rising water levels which impeded extractive activity in British mines—coal as well as other minerals. It seems equally fitting and proper that the British are currently performing the pioneering work in the development of techniques for the instrument-landing of airplanes in dense fog; and conditions of the natural environment make it appropriate for the Israelis to be devoting much effort to cheap desalination techniques, the Dutch to the development of salt-resistant crop varieties, and the students at California Institute of Technology to the attempt to perfect an electric motor for use in automobiles. In all these cases, technological exploration is intimately linked up with patterns of resource availability or conditions of the natural environment in particular locational contexts.[19] But, it is important to add, although the demand or need for a particular kind of technique is established in relation to some aspect of the natural environment, the capacity to respond creatively to this need is an altogether different matter. Past history and the contemporary world abound, to put it mildly, in unsolved problems. Moreover, the *kind* of solution which any society can produce to the problems presented by its natural environment will turn on the level of knowledge and expertise which is available to it. Thus, the Israeli kibbutz with its sophisticated irrigation techniques represents a very different response to the barrenness of the Negev from that of the Arab bedouins;[20] and

19. A recent study of Japanese science fits neatly into the argument presented here: "How good is Japanese science? . . . Perhaps the most reliable guide is a 'self-evaluation' published in the English-language magazine *Technical Japan*. Based on answers to a questionnaire sent to various Japanese science institutes and societies, the survey concluded that Japan excels in subjects where the object of research is either peculiar to or abundant in Japan, such as volcanoes, encephalitis, rice blight, and astronomy; in subjects related to state-run enterprises, such as train operation, magnetometry, and microwave research; in subjects related to industries peculiar to Japan, such as silkworm genetics and zymogenic microorganisms; and in studies related to Japanese industries which compete in international markets, such as shipbuilding, textiles and vitamin synthesis. . . ." "Japan (I): On the Threshold of an Age of Big Science?" *Science*, 2 January 1970, p. 32.

20. The Negev has suffered for centuries from bedouin mismanagement, i.e., continuous overgrazing. However, this desert once supported a sophisticated agricultural system which ingeniously exploited the runoff water from the infrequent and modest rainfalls. For a fascinating account of the work of these

the Ifugao tribesmen of northern Luzon increased rice output for over a thousand years by expanding their extraordinary labor-intensive system of mountain rice terraces, whereas not far from these terraces today farmers are expanding output by exploiting the new, high-yielding rice varieties which have been made possible by modern genetics and botany. Although the "slash and burn" system of agriculture, widely practiced in the humid tropics, permits a limited population to eke out a precarious existence (always provided that natural fertility is restored by sufficiently long fallow periods), a sophisticated knowledge of soil chemistry may pinpoint the soil nutrients which might permit continuous cultivation and far higher levels of output per acre.[21]

Finally, it should be pointed out that the distinction between innovation and adaptation (or between a shift in a production function and movement along an existing production function) is frequently much overstated. It is a common practice among

Nabatean water engineers, see Michael Evenari, Leslie Shanan and Naphtali Tadmor, *The Negev: The Challenge of a Desert* (Cambridge, Mass.: Harvard University Press, 1971), especially chap. VII.

21. "Primitive peoples have knowledge of techniques of accommodation to deserts and jungles that are not commonly commanded by the inhabitants of the high-income regions of the world. Their incomes are higher because they possess this knowledge than they would be in its absence; but the hypothesis can be ventured that they are among the low-income-earning people of the world partly because they are confronted by inhospitable environments, but mainly because they do not possess the classes of knowledge the increments of which earn Nobel awards. In other words, it is here ventured that economic growth and high levels of income are correlated with the possession of the kinds of 'facts and information' that are produced by what has conventionally come to be called 'basic research.' A community that commands a large stock of knowledge of this kind finds applied uses for it. Such a community possesses also a large stock of cognate knowledge that complements other resources and cheapens the cost of production." Simon Rottenberg, "The International Exchange of Knowledge," in C. Arnold Anderson and Mary Jean Bowman (eds.), *Education and Economic Development* (Chicago: Aldine Publishing Company, 1965), p. 282.

economists to draw smooth continuous curves (as we have done) to represent the spectrum of techniques available at a given time. Frequently, however, only a very limited number of points among such possibilities is actually known. Or, it is often the case that a product can be created under carefully controlled laboratory conditions but cannot be produced in commercial quantities without a great deal of further research and engineering. Under these circumstances, the exploratory activity induced by changes in factor prices is of a sort requiring high levels of skill and insight fully comparable to what is ordinarily described as innovation. To call such extensions of the production function, in response to changing factor prices, "adaptations" or "adjustments" but not "innovation" is to understate the technological uncertainties, the creative skills, and the considerable financial cost which such activities frequently involve.

CHAPTER II

The Economic Matrix

AMERICA'S FACTOR ENDOWMENT

In the United States, perhaps the most enduring and pervasive influence shaping the contours of technological development has been the very high land-labor ratio: the abundance of natural resources generally relative to a small population size. A distinctive feature of much American innovation, therefore, was that it was directed toward making possible the exploitation of a large quantity of such resources with relatively little labor, or that it substituted units of the abundant input—natural resources—for units of the scarce input—labor (and, to a lesser extent, capital). For example, a major thrust of agricultural innovation in the second half of the nineteenth century was to increase the acreage which could be cultivated by a single farmer, in large measure by substituting animal power for manpower. In his study of cereal production (wheat, corn, and oats) William Parker found that output per worker in the U.S. more than tripled between 1840 and 1911. Some sixty percent of this increase he attributes in turn to mechanization, a process which raised the feasible acreage-worker ratio, and virtually all of the growth in productivity can be explained by the combination of mechanization with the westward expansion of agriculture.[1] The major improvements came in the harvesting and post-harvesting operations—previously highly labor-intensive activities. In fact, Parker found that seventy percent of the total gain from mechanization was attributable to just two innovations, the reaper and the thresher.[2] In corn production, the replacement of the hoe by the cultivator in the middle decades of the nineteenth century and the introduction of the corn picker in the 1890s were responsible for major reductions in labor requirements. In the South, the cotton gin attacked the highly labor-intensive activity of the manual removal of the seeds from the cotton ball after the cotton had been picked, and thus eliminated a basic constraint upon the westward spread of cotton cultivation in the southern states. Before the development of the cotton gin, production had been confined to seacoast areas where it was possible to grow the long-stranded sea-island cotton. The cotton gin, by sharply reducing the cost of seed removal, made it economically feasible to raise the short-staple upland cotton. With this innovation, cotton culture could be

1. Of course the growth in agricultural productivity due to westward expansion and increasing regional specialization was, in turn, dependent upon improvements in transport facilities. Indeed, by the end of the nineteenth century the railroad, the iron steamship, and refrigeration had gone far beyond national borders and created a high degree of regional agricultural specialization on an international scale. See A. J. Youngson, "The Opening of New Territories," ch. 3 in M. M. Postan and H. J. Habakkuk (eds.), *The Cambridge Economic History of Europe, Vol. VI: The Industrial Revolutions and After* (Cambridge: Cambridge University Press, 1965).

2. W. N. Parker and J. L. V. Klein, "Productivity Growth in Grain Production in the U.S., 1840–60 and 1900–10," in Dorothy S. Brady (ed.), *Output, Employment and Productivity in the U.S. after 1800* (New York: National Bureau of Economic Research, 1966), pp. 523–582. For a description of the major innovations before 1860 see Percy W. Bidwell and John I. Falconer, *History of Agriculture in the Northern U.S., 1620–1860* (Washington D.C.: Carnegie Institution of Washington, 1925), chaps. 13 and 23.

extended far beyond its earlier coastal confinements. Later in the nineteenth century the introduction of cheap barbed-wire fencing in the West—an area with few natural materials for that purpose—made practicable the highly land-intensive techniques of raising livestock which became so characteristic of the region.

In order to exploit the vast forest resources of the country, the United States in the first half of the nineteenth century brought to an advanced stage of perfection a whole range of woodworking machines for sawing, planing, mortising, tenoning, shaping, and boring, in addition to innumerable specialized machines (and in addition to important improvements in the design of that much more venerable instrument, the axe—both head and handle).[3] If manufacturing sectors are ranked by value added by manufacture, the lumber industry in 1860 was, according to the U.S. Census of that year, the second largest industry in the U.S., after cotton goods. In the western and southern states it was the most important manufacturing industry.[4] During this same period per capita lumber consumption in the United States may have been as much as five times as high as in England and Wales.

3. The extent of the use of specialized machinery in woodworking was a source of great surprise to English visitors in the 1850s. One such visitor noted: "Many works in various towns are occupied exclusively in making doors, window frames, or staircases by means of self-acting machinery, such as planing, tenoning, mortising, and jointing machines. They are able to supply builders with the various parts of the woodwork required in buildings at a much cheaper rate than they can produce them in their own workshops without the aid of such machinery. In one of these manufactories twenty men were making panelled doors at the rate of 100 per day." *Special Report of Joseph Whitworth on the New York Industrial Exhibition*, 1854, as reprinted in Nathan Rosenberg (ed.), *The American System of Manufactures* (Edinburgh: University of Edinburgh Press, 1969), p. 344.

4. The 1860 Census of Manufactures states that there were 19,699 establishments in the U.S. engaged in sawing lumber.

By the 1850s American woodworking machinery was generally acknowledged by Europeans to be the most sophisticated and ingenious in the world. The relatively limited degree to which these machines were adopted in Europe, however, seems to have reflected the fact that they were, in many ways, wasteful of wood—a consideration much less important in the United States than in Great Britain in the first half of the nineteenth century. American circular saws, for example, while very fast, had thicker blades, with their teeth spaced widely apart, and converted a distressingly large portion of the log into sawdust. They also generally used more power and required less care and maintenance effort—characteristics well-adapted to American resource endowment but ill-adapted to conditions in the British Isles.[5] Indeed, an observer, writing in the early 1870s, who was intimately familiar with British and American woodworking methods, stated categorically that: "Lumber manufacture, from the log to the finished state, is, in America, characterized by a waste that can truly be called criminal. . . ."[6] This characterization might have been reasonable had American techniques been employed in Britain. Given the relative factor scarcities in the United States, however, these techniques, by substituting cheap wood for expensive labor, may well have been optimal. In England, by contrast, handicraft technology, which amounted to the substitution of (relatively) cheap labor for (relatively) expensive wood continued to prevail.

A similar profligacy in wood consumption persisted within the household so long as wood supplies were locally abundant.

5. Because of their much more rapid action, woodworking machines employed considerably more power than metal-working machines.

6. J. Richards, *A Treatise on the Construction and Operation of Woodworking Machines* (London, 1872), p. 141.

Under these circumstances, fireplaces were designed to accommodate large logs, an arrangement which was wasteful of fuel wood but economized upon the labor-intensive activities of cutting or chopping wood. As local supplies were exhausted and wood became more costly, stoves, which utilized wood supplies more efficiently but required more labor inputs in preparing the wood, gradually replaced the fireplace. At the same time, as the nineteenth century progressed, more and more attention was devoted to improvements in stove design, primarily in New England and the Middle Atlantic states.[7]

America's abundance of resources led to many other adaptations which would have struck a European observer as wasteful, but which in fact constituted a substitution of natural resources for other, scarcer, factors of production. The abundance of wood, for example, led to its utilization in ways which astonished European visitors to the United States in the first half of the nineteenth century. The American builder relied on wood in uses where his European counterpart would have employed stone, iron, or other materials. In the construction of housing, this led to the development in the 1830s of a uniquely American technique of housebuilding: the highly utilitarian balloon-frame design. Balloon frame houses employed much lighter framing than traditional houses, having systematically eliminated the larger beams and other heavy members of traditional New England houses, a difference which reduced the number of workers required on the housing site. Such houses, moreover, eliminated the highly labor-intensive mortising and tenoning

7. The U.S. Patent Office issued over 800 patents for stoves between 1790 and 1845, and in 1846 it was reported by the Patent Office that it had more models of stoves than of any other single class of objects. A. William Hoglund, "Forest Conservation and Stove Inventors—1789–1850," *Forest History*, Winter 1962, p. 6.

procedures which were previously required, and they were nailed together with light 2″ × 4″ studs.[8] Their lightness, simplicity, and flexibility of design sharply reduced labor requirements in housing construction. But, in addition to housing, Americans made extensive use of wood materials in other, more improbable uses: not only in building bridges and aqueducts, but even in roads (plank roads), pavements, the framing of steam engines, and canal locks.[9] For not only was wood an

8. Carl W. Condit, *American Building* (Chicago: University of Chicago Press, 1968), pp. 43–45. It should be noted also that as early as 1800 the United States had already taken the lead in replacing the hand-wrought nail with one cut by machinery. Nail prices declined sharply in the years after 1817.

9. A British engineer, visiting America in the late 1830s, made the following observations on American canal construction: "At the first view, one is struck with the temporary and apparently unfinished state of many of the American works, and is very apt, before inquiring into the subject, to impute to want of ability what turns out, on investigation, to be a judicious and ingenious arrangement to suit the circumstances of a new country, of which the climate is severe, —a country where stone is scarce and wood is plentiful, and where manual labour is very expensive. It is vain to look to the American works for the finish that characterises those of France, or the stability for which those of Britain are famed. Undressed slopes of cuttings and embankments, roughly built rubble arches, stone parapet-walls coped with timber, and canal-locks wholly constructed of that material, every where offend the eye accustomed to view European workmanship. But it must not be supposed that this arises from want of knowledge of the principles of engineering, or of skill to do them justice in the execution. The use of wood, for example, which may be considered by many as wholly inapplicable to the construction of canal-locks, where it must not only encounter the tear and wear occasioned by the lockage of vessels, but must be subject to the destructive consequences of alternate immersion in water and exposure to the atmosphere, is yet the result of deliberate judgment. The Americans have, in many cases, been induced to use the material of the country, ill adapted though it be in some respects to the purposes to which it is applied, in order to meet the wants of a rising community, by speedily and perhaps superficially completing a work of importance, which would otherwise be delayed, from a want of the means to execute it in a more substantial manner; and although the works are wanting in finish, and even in solidity, they do not fail for many years to serve the purposes for which they were constructed, as efficiently as works of a more lasting description." David Stevenson, *Sketch of the Civil Engineering of North America* (London, 1838), pp. 192–193.

abundant and widely distributed material in the eastern half of the United States, but its use quite generally reduced the labor requirements of construction activity.

SOME FACTORS UNDERLYING INNOVATIVE ACTIVITY

Technological change, as we have seen, can be examined as an adaptive, problem-solving process whereby techniques are developed which enable a society to exploit the opportunities and to overcome the constraints implicit in a particular environment. More than this, it seems fair to state that economic growth reflects the success which a country has had in mobilizing its resources in achieving the technological breakthroughs essential for economic success in a particular environment. In saying this, it is clear that we are raising questions which go far beyond the realm of conventional economics and involve questions of human skills, motivation, and the efficiency of social and economic institutions. Why do some societies have a much greater apparent *capacity* to generate the appropriate inventions than do others? Why are some societies much more receptive to the introduction of inventions made elsewhere? These are very different questions, for the requirements for successful inventive activity may be very different from the requirements for the rapid *adoption* of an invention, once it has been made. Whereas the former question involves the supply of inventive talent, originality, and the ability to apply specialized knowledge to the solution of technical problems, the latter question is more likely to turn upon the supply of managerial abilities, highly motivated entrepreneurs, business acumen, and organizational effectiveness. Indeed, it has often been said of the

French that they had great inventive talent but that French society was not equally well-suited for the rapid application of new inventions;[10] whereas it has often been observed that, although the Japanese have not been responsible for many major inventions, they have had a remarkable capacity for exploiting foreign inventions for their own purposes.[11]

In the case of the United States in the nineteenth century, the rapid rate of technological change reflected both a high level of inventive activity and a rapid rate of adoption. The United States, it should be remembered, possessed the advantages of all latecomers of being able to borrow and to modify a technology which had been developed by others. Immigrants to the United States brought European technology with them and continued to draw heavily upon it. Furthermore, the intensity of energy and single-mindedness of purpose with which Americans pursued their economic goals has long been a matter of common notoriety. Doubtless the large flow of immigrants into American society had a good deal to do with the strong economic

10. "The most striking contrast between Britain and France at this period [early nineteenth century] is the higher rate at which, in Britain, inventions were adopted, developed and passed into application. No nation in the world showed more vivid inventive genius than the French, but a high proportion of their inventive talent proved abortive or was put to profitable use elsewhere —notably in England and Scotland." Charles Wilson, "Technology and Industrial Organization," in Charles Singer et al. (eds.) *A History of Technology* (Oxford: Clarendon Press, 1958), vol. V, p. 800.

11. Recent studies by the OECD of technological innovations since 1945 conclude that Europe, by comparison with the U.S.A., is relatively more efficient at inventing than it is at innovating. These studies indicate a decisive superiority for the U.S., as compared to Europe, at the critical stage of transforming an invention into a commercially viable and profitable product. OECD, *Gaps in Technology, Analytical Report* (Paris, 1970), Book 3. Moreover, as this study also points out: "The pattern of performance in innovation within the various industrial sectors is probably more revealing. It suggests that United States' performance in originating innovations is particularly strong in new product groups with rapid rates of technological change." *Ibid.*, p. 199.

orientation of the American population. It seems a reasonable conjecture that the Europeans who migrated to the United States did not constitute a random sample of the European population; rather, they must have been a selective group (they obviously were a self-*selected* group), including a predominance of those who were more highly responsive to economic incentives and prepared to experience privation and uncertainties and to endure the strangeness of a new culture and environment so long as it held out the prospect of eventual economic improvement.

The strong utilitarian bent in American society was described as follows in an article "Forty Days in a Western Hotel" which appeared in *Putnam's Magazine* in December 1854:

The genius of this new country is necessarily mechanical. Our greatest thinkers are not in the library, nor the capitol, but in the machine shop. The American people is intent on studying, not the beautiful records of a past civilization, not the hieroglyphic monuments of ancient genius, but how best to subdue and till the soil of its boundless territories; how to build roads and ships; how to apply the powers of nature to the work of manufacturing its rich materials into forms of utility and enjoyment. The youth of this country are learning the sciences, not as theories, but with reference to their application to the arts. Our education is no genial culture of letters, but simply learning the use of tools.[12]

12. The article, by J. Milton Mackie, was published anonymously but reprinted later in Mackie's book, *From Cape Cod to Dixie and the Tropics* (New York, 1864), pp. 200–201 of the book. Thomas Jefferson, himself a scientist of some note, stressed the utilitarian role of science in a letter to Thomas Cooper in 1812: "You know the just esteem which attached itself to Dr. Franklin's science, because he always endeavored to direct it to something useful in private life. The chemists have not been attentive enough to this. I have wished to see their science applied to domestic objects, to malting, for instance, brewing, making cider, to fermentation and distillation generally, to the making of bread, butter, cheese, soap, to the incubation of eggs, etc. And I am happy to observe some of these titles in the syllabus of your lecture. I hope you will make the chemistry of these subjects intelligible to our good housewives." Thomas Jefferson to Thomas Cooper, July 10, 1812, Andrew A. Lipscomb (ed.), *The Writings of Thomas Jefferson*, 20 vols. (Washington, D.C.: 1903–1904), 13: 176–

Mackie undoubtedly well expresses certain attitudes and values which had a good deal to do with the high rate of technological change in the nineteenth century.[13] These positive social values, as well as the absence of inhibiting institutions which were prevalent in Europe, cooperated to direct much of the creative energy of the American population into pursuits which often resulted in the development of new and superior techniques.

177. As quoted in Hugo Meier, "Technology and Democracy, 1800–1860," *Mississippi Valley Historical Review*, 43 (1957): 622.

13. America's limited interest in basic science and preoccupation, in earlier days, with its purely practical aspects had been pointed out by Tocqueville: "It must be acknowledged that in few of the civilized nations of our time have the higher sciences made less progress than in the United States. . . . The mind may, as it appears to me, divide science into three parts. The first comprises the most theoretical principles, and those more abstract notions, whose application is either unknown or very remote. The second is composed of those general truths which still belong to pure theory, but lead nevertheless by a straight and short road to practical results. Methods of application and means of execution make up the third. Each of these different portions of science may be separately cultivated, although reason and experience prove that neither of them can prosper long, if it be absolutely cut off from the two others. In America, the purely practical part of science is admirably understood and careful attention is paid to the theoretical portion, which is immediately requisite to application. On this head, the Americans always display a clear, free, original, and inventive power of mind. But hardly any one in the United States devotes himself to the essentially theoretical and abstract portion of human knowledge . . . every new method which leads by a shorter road to wealth, every machine which spares labor, every instrument which diminishes the cost of production, every discovery which facilitates pleasures or augments them, seems [to such people] to be the grandest effort of the human intellect. It is chiefly from these motives that a democratic people addicts itself to scientific pursuits. . . . In a community thus organized, it may easily be conceived that the human mind may be led insensibly to the neglect of theory; and that it is urged, on the contrary, with unparalleled energy, to the applications of science, or at least to that portion of theoretical science which is necessary to those who make such applications. In vain will some instinctive inclination raise the mind towards the loftier spheres of the intellect; interest draws it down to the middle zone. There it may develop all its energy and restless activity, and bring forth wonders." Alexis de Tocqueville, *Democracy in America* (New York: The Century Co., 1898), vol. 2, pp. 40, 48, 52–53.

Not only did American society devote a large proportion of its resources to inventive activities; it is also apparent that the human resources of the country were well-equipped through formal education with the skills which might raise their productivity both as inventors and as successful borrowers and modifiers of technologies developed elsewhere. The long-standing nature of the American commitment to education is apparent in Table 1.

As early as 1830 the proportion of the population enrolled in school in the United States was second only to that of Germany. Since the institution of slavery in the United States effectively set at zero the educational opportunities available to a significant proportion of the population, it is probably true that the white American population of 1830 would have ranked first by the (admittedly crude) measure of Table 1. In 1850 the American figures for school enrollment were unqualifiedly the highest of all those available and, by that date, the white American population was among the best educated, if not *the* best educated, in the world. Moreover, the figures for the New England states, where much of the inventive activity was concentrated, were substantially above the national average. Clearly this commitment to education was a major conditioning factor and was of far-reaching significance in its effects upon invention and diffusion.[14]

14. A study of member countries of the Organization for Economic Cooperation and Development shows that the U.S. in 1964 was spending a higher percentage of her GNP on education—6.2%—than any of the other member countries. Italy, The Netherlands, Sweden, Canada, and Japan were all over 5%, The United Kingdom was just below 5%, Belgium and France were both 4.3%, and Germany lagged behind at 3.4%. In the earlier pre-sputnik year, 1955, the U.S. figure was 4.1%, placing her below Japan and Sweden, both of which were devoting 4.4% of their GNP in that year to educational expenditure. OECD, *Gaps in Technology, op. cit.*, p. 32, Table 9.

.For a perceptive examination of the reasons for America's superiority over Western Europe in bringing the apparatus of scientific research and higher

Moreover, the easy access to education in the United States provided a route by which the ambitious and able could readily move out of their humble beginnings. In this sense the educational system was important, not only because it equipped individuals with useful skills but also because it increased social mobility and thereby raised the probability that talented people would reach positions where society would effectively utilize these talents. Education, from this point of view, assured a more efficient allocation of human resources. This point was not lost on English visitors.

The successful application of mechanical means to one manufacture has been, as a matter of course, stimulative of their application to another, however different, and the adaptive versatility of an educated people was never more fully displayed than in the constant effort to supply their greatest want—that of skilled labour—by applications of mechanical powers to that object. Nor can the most superficial observer fail to be impressed with the advantages thus derived from the long and well-directed attention paid to the education of the whole people by the public school systems of the New England States and of the State of Pennsylvania. Here, where sound and systematic education has been longest and, in all probability, most perfectly carried out, the greatest manufacturing developments are to be found, and here it is also where the greatest portion of the skilled workmen of the United States are educated, alike in the simplest elements of knowledge, as in the most skilful application of their ingenuity to the useful arts and the manufacturing industry of their country, and from whence they are spread over the vast territories of the Union, becoming the originators, directors, and, ultimately, the proprietors of establishments which would do no discredit to the manufacturing States of Europe.[15]

education to bear upon problems of importance to the national economy, see Joseph Ben-David, *Fundamental Research and the Universities* (Paris: OECD, 1968).

15. *New York Industrial Exhibition. Special Report of Mr. George Wallis*, as reprinted in Rosenberg, *op. cit.*, p. 203.

Although it is difficult to say a great deal in purely economic terms about national differences in inventiveness and the capacity for "creative responses," basic economic reasoning is an indispensable guide in attempting to answer more modest questions concerning the path of historical change. Earlier it was suggested that the search for new techniques was strongly influenced by conditions of the natural environment, and factor endowment generally, which inevitably pose specific constraints and provide specific opportunities for participants in the economic arena. It is now time that we recognize explicitly the economic content of these assertions. Inventive activity, after all, involves the use of scarce and valuable resources which have a wide range of alternative uses, and therefore even on purely a priori grounds one would not expect to find such resources distributed in a random way among the different sectors of the economy. Like other economic activities, inventive activity is responsive to market forces and the prospects of financial gain. These prospects for financial gain which shape the allocation of inventive effort can be resolved into demand forces and supply forces which determine the expected "payoff" to a successful inventive effort.[16] Inventive activity may be visualized as a pursuit which receives its changing direction over time from the changing perceptions of future profits (profit expectations) which are attached to the solution of spe-

16. Since inventive activity is fundamentally a learning process, the outcomes of such activity are not known with certainty. This means that the return to expenditures on this activity may be a random variable, and choice criteria under uncertainty must be used to evaluate the probability distribution of possible returns. For an enlightening discussion of the nature of research and development in terms of Bayesian probability, see Kenneth Arrow, "Classificatory Notes on the Production and Transmission of Technological Knowledge," *American Economic Review, Papers and Proceedings*, May 1969, pp. 29–35.

Table 1

Estimated Percentage of Total Population (All Ages) Enrolled in School, in Various Countries 1830–1928

	1830	1850	1887	1928
United States	15	18	22	24
England and Wales	9 }	12	16	16
Scotland		—	16	17
Ireland		7	14	18
Australia	6	—	14	16
Germany	17	16	18	17
Switzerland	13	—	18	—
Netherlands	12	13	14	19
Denmark	14 }	—	12	16
Norway		14	13	17
Sweden		13	15	13
France	7	10	15	11
Austria	5 }	7	13	14
Hungary			12	16
Italy	3	—	11	11
Spain	4	—	11	11
Portugal	—	1	5	6
Greece	—	5	6	12
Russia/USSR	—	2	3	12

Source: Richard A. Easterlin, "A Note on the Evidence of History," in C. Arnold Anderson and Mary Jean Bowman (eds.), *Education and Economic Development* (Chicago: Aldine Publishing Company, 1965; London, Frank Cass & Company, 1966), pp. 426–427. Reprinted by permission of Aldine-Atherton, Inc. and Frank Cass and Company Limited.

cific technical problems. Since the activity is rooted in the perception of future profit possibilities, it will be influenced by any forces which (1) alter the revenue flow which the use of the invention is expected to generate or which, (2) alter the expected cost of making the invention.

THE ROLE OF DEMAND

Thus, on the demand side, the "need" for any given invention will be influenced by (a) any increase in revenue flows, or (b) any reduction in expenditure flows associated with the employment of the invention. The expected returns to an invention, then, will be affected by any of the forces which alter the demand for the final product to which the invention may be related. Such forces might include changes in per capita income, changes in family size and age composition of the population, urbanization, etc. It has been demonstrated in an authoritative way that variations in demand-pull forces are a major determinant of variations in the allocation of inventive effort to specific industries. In examining the railroad industry for which comprehensive data are available for over a century, Schmookler found a close correspondence between increases in the purchase of railroad equipment and components, and slightly lagged increases in patenting activity (see Chart 1). Similarly, reductions in the purchase of railroad equipment were followed by a lagged decline in patenting activity. The lag, Schmookler argues, indicates that it is variations in the sale of equipment which induce the variations in patenting. Schmookler finds similar relationships in building and petroleum refining, although the long-term data on these industries are less comprehensive. Furthermore, and equally important, in examining cross-sectional data for a large number of industries in the years before and after the Second World War, Schmookler finds a very high correlation between capital goods inventions in an industry and the volume of sales of capital goods to that industry.[17] Schmookler's empirical data, therefore, strongly support the view that inventors perceive the growth in the purchase of equipment by an industry as signalling an expansion of profit prospects in that industry, and direct their talents accordingly. Thus, Schmookler concludes that, both in the short run and the long run, demand considerations—through their influence upon the size of the market for particular classes of inventions—are the decisive determinant of the allocation of inventive effort. Similarly, Griliches has shown that the entry of hybrid corn seed producers into different portions of the national market was closely related to expected demand, as measured by each region's market density.[18]

The demand for, and the profitability of, specific kinds of inventions may change in response to numerous forces, including economic growth itself. The much higher levels of per capita incomes today as compared to the early nineteenth century, and the differences in the composition of expenditures associated with higher levels of income (Engel's Law), have a great deal to do with the preoccupation with invention in food preparation and processing 150 years ago as contrasted with the much greater importance of inventions oriented toward leisure-time activities today. The cutting off of traditional overseas sources of supply during wartime sharply increased the demand for, and the profitability of, close substitutes, as suggested

17. Jacob Schmookler, *Invention and Economic Growth* (Cambridge, Mass.: Harvard University Press, 1966).
18. Zvi Griliches, "Hybrid Corn: An Exploration in the Economics of Technological Change," *Econometrica*, October 1957, pp. 506–515.

Chart 1

Capital Formation and Patents in the Railroad Industry, 1840–1950

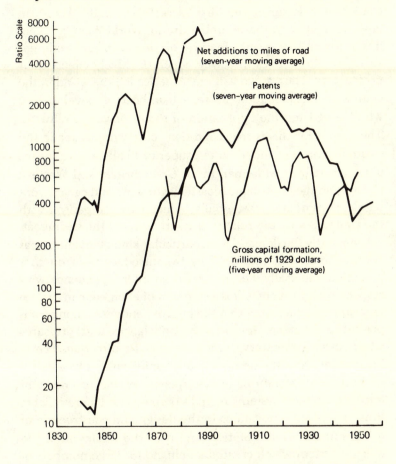

Source: Jacob Schmookler, "Changes in Industry and the State of Knowledge as Determinants of Industrial Invention," in *The Rate and Direction of Inventive Activity*, National Bureau of Economic Research (Princeton, N.J.: Princeton University Press, 1962), p. 200. Reprinted by permission of the National Bureau of Economic Research.

Net additions to miles of roads are used as representative of capital formation for the early years when a more direct measure is not available.

earlier (recall the German development of the Haber nitrogen fixation process during the First World War and the American development of synthetic rubber during World War II). Again, it is apparent that specific features of the natural environment structure alternatives in a way which decisively affects their profitability. Thus, as we will see, America led the world in the commercial exploitation of the steamboat, a development which antedated the application of steam power to railways. The reason for this is that conditions of geography made the steamboat, in the United States, superior to alternative means of transport by a wide margin. In Great Britain and Western Europe, on the other hand, coastal waterways and canals were highly efficient and substantially reduced, by comparison with the United States, the relative attractiveness of the steamboat.

Frequently the demand for a particular kind of invention has been generated or increased by the introduction of *another* invention, especially where there is an interdependence with respect to performance. It is a common phenomenon in the use of complex technologies that the interdependence among component parts generates internal imbalances and pressures which push exploratory activity in specific directions. Thus, improvements in the design of automobile engines have led—due to the possibility of higher speeds—to the invention of improved braking systems as well as stronger and more reliable tires. Important innovations in the design and construction of bridges in the United States came with the expansion of the railroad system which created a demand for large numbers of bridges which could meet certain high performance specifications. Similarly on the railroads, Westinghouse's important invention of the air brake occurred after people became seriously concerned over the difficulty of stopping long trains, carrying heavy goods at high speeds, a development which, in turn, had been made possible by the earlier introduction of cheap methods of steel production and the substitution of steel rails for iron rails. Improvements in weaving operations in textiles in eighteenth-century England increased the profitability of inventions in spinning, by increasing the demand for spun yarn. In the machine tool industry just after the turn of the twentieth century, the introduction of high speed steel—a steel alloy which dramatically increased the speed at which machine tools could cut metal—generated numerous changes in the other component parts of the machine tool—the structural, transmission, and control elements—without which the benefits of the high speed steel could not have been fully exploited. For example, the cone pulley, a primitive device for altering the speed of the machine tool in accordance with the requirements of the work in hand, was replaced by much more sophisticated gear-change devices which enabled the operator to vary the speed merely by shifting a lever. Similar sequences of shifting profitability have occurred in recent years along with the introduction of cemented carbide tools and ceramic tools; and the beneficent outcome of this interdependence in the components of the lathe could be duplicated in the relationship between milling cutters and milling machines or grinding wheels and grinding machines. Examples could easily be multiplied where specific kinds of inventions became more profitable—and were eventually forthcoming—because of technical progress in connection with closely related productive processes.

There is another consideration on the side of demand which appears to have been significant in influencing technological change. Anglo-American experience with the introduction and diffusion of technology in the nineteenth century points strongly to the importance of the composition of consumer demand and the extent of malleability of public tastes. The willingness of the public to accept a homogeneous final product was probably a major factor in the transition from a labor-intensive handicraft technology to one involving a sequence of highly specialized machines. Across a whole range of commodities there is evidence that British consumers imposed their tastes on the producer in a manner which seriously constrained him with respect to the exploitation of machine technology. English observers often noted with no small astonishment that American products were designed to accommodate, not the consumer, but the machine. One author notes of the American cutlery trade, for example, that ". . . where mechanical devices cannot be adjusted to the production of the traditional product, the product must be modified to the demands of the machine. Hence, the standard American table-knife is a rigid, metal shape, handle and blade forged in one piece, the whole being finished by electroplating—an implement eminently suited to factory production."[19] Even with respect to an object so ostensibly utilitarian as a gun, the British civilian market was long dominated by peculiarities of taste which essentially precluded machine techniques. In fact, in the 1830s we find a Colonel Hawkins instructing his (presumably upper-class) readers that "The length, bend and casting of a stock [gunstock] must, of course, be fitted to the shooter, who should have his measure for them as carefully entered in a gunmaker's books, as that for a suit of clothes on those of his tailor."[20] Americans, on the other hand, for whom a gun was a simple object of utility, for the dispatch of rodents and farm pests, readily accepted a high degree of standardization. Similarly, America's early leadership

19. G. I. H. Lloyd, *The Cutlery Trades* (London: Longmans, Green and Co., 1913), pp. 394–395.

20. As quoted in *A Treatise on the Progressive Improvement and Present State of the Manufactures in Metal* (London, 1833), vol. II, p. 105.

in mechanizing the production of men's clothing reflected a greater willingness on the American side to accept a "ready-made" suit, or pair of boots or shoes.[21]

These differences in consumer tastes seem to have been related to a much more widespread phenomenon in Britain as compared to the U.S. of what might be called "customer initiative" as opposed to "producer initiative." That is, in America the producer of capital goods took the initiative in matters of machine design and successfully suppressed variations in product design which served no clearly defined purpose. He

21. On the other hand, willingness to accept a standardized, machine-made product should not be confused with indifference to quality or even to changes in fashion. For example, American manufacturers made considerable inroads into traditionally British footwear markets at the end of the nineteenth century before British manufacturers finally grasped this essential point. "Nineteenth-century [British] footwear, whether the product of the wholesale putting-out system or of the early factory, was often badly made and rarely distinguished between left and right; the range of fittings was limited, and in the absence of nationally accepted standards, each manufacturer had his own sizes. At its best, the industry produced a durable boot, of ugly design and rough leather, having tops of thick leather which ridged easily. A deputation of manufacturers to the United States at the beginning of this century was surprised to find that the industry there manufactured in half-sizes, as well as producing a generally superior article. It was not surprising that, during the 'nineties and early part of this century, many customers at home and abroad turned to the superior product of the American and sometimes the European industries. Well into the twentieth century, if the consumer at home, buying British, required anything more than an ill-fitting, uncomfortable black boot, elastic-sided or hobnailed, he turned to the bespoke shoe-maker. However, having learned the lesson from competitors, British manufacturers rapidly put their house in order and around the turn of the century they increasingly adopted improved machinery and refined techniques of production, supplying wider ranges of fittings and paying greater attention to style and the appearance of their product." P. Head, "Boots and Shoes," chap. 6 in Derek H. Aldcroft (ed.), *The Development of British Industry and Foreign Competition, 1875–1914* (Toronto: University of Toronto Press, 1968) p. 183. The belief that high quality was incompatible with mass production techniques long persisted in British industry. Abundant evidence on this point may be found in *Survey of Metal Industries*, Committee on Industry and Trade, pt. 4 (London: HMSO, 1928), pp. 220–221, 227–228, and passim.

brought about, in other words, a high degree of standardization in the machinery, which very much simplified his own production problems, and in turn reduced the price of capital goods. This producer initiative was a very important factor in developing patterns of efficient specialization in American capital goods production.

In England, on the other hand, the capital goods producer remained, to a surprising degree, what Landes has aptly called a "custom tailor working in metal." The explanation for this difference in roles is not entirely clear. In the case of many kinds of capital goods, the variations in machine design were quite unrelated to any functional justification. Buyers of machinery were in the habit of drawing up blueprints with highly detailed specifications which the machine producer had to agree to provide as a condition of fulfillment of the contract. Many of the specifications were often nothing more than the result of historical accident. In England the initiative in matters of machine design was emphatically in the hands of the buyer, and this had serious implications for the machine-producing sector both as a transmission center for the diffusion of new techniques and as a producer of low-cost machinery.[22]

The problems thus encountered by the machinery-producing sector were further intensified by the role of that strange British

22. At the turn of the twentieth century some evidence of change began to appear. A British observer in 1902 made the following highly revealing comments: "Some few years ago no machine-tool maker ventured to offer advice to a manufacturing engineer as to the tools he might buy or the methods he should follow. He would have been told to mind his own business. Today a good deal of help and advice is often requested and the tool maker and user, as they should be, are often in consultation as to tools, methods and organization. Machine tool making in America has been, I take it, considered a reputable business for some years, whereas here for a time it certainly was but little considered." William H. Booth, "An English View of American Tools," *American Machinist*, November 6, 1902, p. 1580.

institution, the consulting engineer. These engineers were imbued with a professional tradition which often led to an obsession with technical perfection in a purely engineering sense, and they imposed their own tastes and idiosyncrasies upon product design. In America, by contrast, the engineer and engineering skills were more effectively subordinated to business discipline and commercial criteria, and did not dominate them.[23] The result was to perpetuate, in Great Britain, a preoccupation with purely technical aspects of the final *product* rather than with the productive *process*.

The balloon-frame houses, mentioned earlier, are an excellent and major example of American willingness to reject aesthetic embellishments and ornamentation in favor of new construction techniques which often horrified Europeans but which satisfied more simple and more purely functionally-oriented tastes.

These balloon-frame buildings were often designed and constructed without reference to any requirements other than those of utility, and they were often appallingly unattractive. Professional architects usually regarded them with horror. To Calvert Vaux, for instance, who, like Gervase Wheeler, had come to the United States with the best available English training and had devoted his life to the realization in this country of his ideals of his art, such houses seemed to have been constructed without any sense of proportion or the slightest apparent desire to make them agreeable objects in the landscape. These "bare, bald white cubes," as he called them in 1857, struck him as monotonous evidence of a life spent "with little or no cultivation of the higher natural perceptions." And like many of his cultivated contemporaries, he set about doing his best to educate the American people in sifting, testing, and improving all suitable architectural forms and modes of the past. He recommends, for instance, Moorish arcades and verandas

23. See, for example, Daniel H. Calhoun, *The American Civil Engineer: Origin and Conflicts* (Cambridge, Mass.: M.I.T. Press, 1960), especially chap. 6.

and Chinese balconies and trellises added to what he calls the "irregular Italian" or to the "later modifications of the Gothic."[24]

It is hardly necessary to add that Vaux's architectural recommendations exerted no significant impact upon American building practices.

Nineteenth-century American society was dominated by the tastes of rural households, relatively prosperous by European standards, with a strong preference for moderately priced household furnishings, durable goods and equipment—cooking equipment, stoves, sewing machines (with which clothing for women and children were manufactured in the home), cabinet furniture, carpets and a wide range of coarse textile fabrics, clocks and watches, china, glassware, etc.[25] Such tastes influenced not only the nature of the final products and, in this way, the productive process; they also exerted a pervasive effect upon the development of techniques of marketing and distribution, as is attested to by the absence, outside of the largest cities, of specialty stores, the prominent role of the general store in rural areas, and the founding of Montgomery Ward and Sears Roebuck at the end of the nineteenth century. Even the Model T Ford may be regarded as the natural mechanized successor to rural America's horse-drawn buggy, which it in fact closely resembled. Indeed, it was rural households which were in the forefront of the adoption of the automobile for private family use in the early days of the automobile industry. Urban

24. John A. Kouwenhoven, *The Arts in Modern American Civilization* (New York: W. W. Norton, 1967), p. 52. This book was originally published in 1948 under the title *Made in America*.

25. For a further discussion of this point, see Dorothy Brady, "The Content of the National Product," which appears as chap. 3 in Lance E. Davis, et al., *American Economic Growth: An Economist's History of the United States* (New York: Harper & Row, 1971).

families were, by and large, equipped with reasonable public transportation alternatives.

The high degree of standardization of goods in America may be regarded as, in part, an economically efficient way of catering to the needs of a highly dispersed, relatively affluent rural society for whom customized, individualized production was usually not a feasible alternative. Because of the large size of their holdings, American farmers did not live clustered together in a village community as in Europe, but spread out over a broad terrain in farmstead residences. It is important to remember that it was only in the twentieth century that America came to constitute a predominantly urban society and was overwhelmingly rural in the nineteenth century. In 1800 barely 6 percent of the population was urban and in 1860 the figure was still under 20 percent. This figure rose rapidly in the post-Civil War decades, but even in 1900, 60 percent of the population was still classified as rural.[26] The growing dominance of urban culture and life styles in twentieth-century rural America in fact owed a great deal to the superior mobility provided by the automobile and, later, to electricity. The latter served, quite literally, to "plug in" the farm family to the increasingly dominant urban culture after the automobile had made this culture more easily accessible to it.

There seems to have been an intimate relationship, then, between the composition of demand and homogeneity of product, on the one hand, and the range of technological possibilities open to society, on the other. In order to be suitable for mass production techniques, the producer must be free to design his

26. *Historical Statistics of the United States, Colonial Times to 1957* (U.S. Bureau of the Census, Washington, D.C., 1960), p. 14. The census definition here includes as rural population all persons living in communities of less than 2,500 inhabitants.

product with some minimum degree of freedom, and it seems apparent that, in this respect, the American producer was much less constrained by the nature of consumer tastes than was his English counterpart. Americans readily accepted products which had been deliberately designed or modified in such a way as to make them suitable for low cost, mass production methods. This difference had a great deal to do with the fact that mass production technology essentially originated in the United States rather than in England and with early American leadership in products which were particularly well suited to such techniques. The distinctive nature of American goods, as they were exhibited at the London Crystal Palace Exhibition in 1851, was perceptively noted by British observers in the official catalogue:

The absence in the United States of those vast accumulations of wealth which favour the expenditure of large sums on articles of mere luxury, and the general distribution of the means of procuring the more substantial conveniences of life, impart to the productions of American industry a character distinct from that of many other countries. The expenditure of months or years of labour upon a single article, not to increase its intrinsic value, but solely to augment its cost or its estimation as an object of *virtu*, is not common in the United States. On the contrary, both manual and mechanical labour are applied with direct reference to increasing the number or the quantity of articles suited to the wants of a whole people, and adapted to promote the enjoyment of that moderate competency which prevails among them.[27]

Indeed, the American exhibit offered very little to visitors who came to gratify their aesthetic sensibilities. They were far better served at the adjacent Russian, Austrian, and French exhibits, which offered abundant displays of works of artistic

27. *Official Description and Illustrated Catalogue of the Great Exhibition of the Works of Industry of All Nations* (London, 1851), vol. III, p. 1431.

merit (however meretricious these items may appear to us to-day). But the severely utilitarian nature of the American display, containing objects which catered to simple and specific human needs, and possessing no ornamental value whatever, surely epitomized much about the nature of American society. Characteristic of the American exhibit were its ice-making machines, corn-husk mattresses, fireproofed safes, meat biscuits, india-rubber shoes and lifeboats, railroad switches, nautical instruments, telegraph instruments, a special grease-removing soap which was usable either with salt or fresh water, artificial arms and legs and, far from least, agricultural machinery.

THE ROLE OF SUPPLY

So far the discussion of the determinants of the direction of inventive activity has been confined to demand side forces. But clearly demand side forces alone can no more explain the allocation of inventive resources than they can, alone, provide an explanation for the determination of the price of a commodity.[28] For such an explanation we must consider, also, the role of supply side phenomena. The basic argument is that, at any time, demand and supply considerations interact to provide, for the whole range of inventive possibilities, a configuration of profit expectations which, in turn, shape the allocation of inventive resources. Furthermore, changes in the allocation of such resources over time may result from a shift in the structure of demand, a shift in the structure of supply, or both. A

---

28. Hotspur's decisive riposte made an analogous point in act III, scene I of *Henry IV, Part I:*
"Glendower: I can call spirits from the vasty deep.
Hotspur: Why, so can I, or so can any man; but will they come when you do call for them?"

comprehensive treatment of the path of historical change with respect to inventive activity would explain such changes in terms of the specific forces underlying movements in demand or supply schedules. But it is fair to say that, from a long run perspective, economic growth involves a progressive relaxation of supply side constraints, a continual outward shifting of supply schedules. In the short run, on the other hand, the nature of the supply side constraints must be explored in order to understand the specific direction of inventive activity. People possessing technical skills inevitably work on problems which their knowledge and training render interesting and potentially soluble (and therefore potentially rewarding). Such people devote their attention only to some rather small subset of the universe of potential inventions which would, if successfully developed, prove rewarding. Therefore supply considerations, broadly considered, determine the repertoire of responses to demand forces which are within the capacity of a society at any given time.

What can be said about the role of supply? Clearly, the prospective cost of an invention will depend upon the supply of all the factors involved in inventive activity. Such costs, therefore, will reflect the scarcity or abundance of these factors and, in addition, any qualitative aspects which are relevant for the inventive process. The capacity to solve certain problems, which is the essence of inventive activity, will depend upon the supply of labor possessing the requisite human skills, training, and talents, whether acquired through apprenticeship, on-the-job training, or formal education; and upon the state of organized technological and scientific knowledge which can be made available to potential inventors. The supplies of the human and nonhuman inputs combine to determine, at any given time, the production functions, and therefore the prospective costs, for particular inventions. *Changes* in these human and nonhuman inputs over time are responsible for differential shifts in the production functions for different categories of human wants, or for different ways of satisfying the same want or the same category of wants. Improvements in the appropriate skills, talents, and knowledge combine to lower the expected cost, and therefore to raise the expected profitability, of a particular inventive effort.

Here, as in our earlier discussion, it is important that the realm of discourse be shifted from the abstract and general to the particular and specific. For technological change is not something which has emerged in a random way from all sectors of the economy. It is, rather, the result of certain acquired problem-solving skills which, in our history, have been heavily concentrated in some specific sectors of the economy. Throughout the early stages of American industrialization—throughout the entire nineteenth century, although with decreasing emphasis toward the end of the century—these skills were heavily concentrated in metallurgy, machine tools, steam power, and engineering; later, in large part as a result of advances in science, this focus shifted to chemistry-based, electrical- and electronics-based, and more recently biology-based industries. With the dramatic growth of these science-based industries in the twentieth century, technological change has become increasingly dependent upon the exploitation of scientific knowledge—often knowledge of recent acquisition. Thus, the development of hybrid corn in the 1930s required a sophisticated knowledge of genetic processes; the post-World War II development of the transistor was made possible by quantum mechanics as it emerged in the 1920s; and the spectacular growth in synthetic materials was built upon an advanced understanding of molecular chemistry. This growing intimacy between scientific and technological advances in certain industries is a very recent phenomenon, and has been associated with drastic organizational and institutional changes on the supply side in recent decades. Indeed, when Mendelejeff published his periodic table of the elements in 1869, there was not a single journal devoted to the subject of chemistry in the United States. Until the 1870s, the major publication outlet for American chemistry was the *American Journal of Science,* which had been founded by Benjamin Silliman, Sr., in 1818, and which catered to the whole range of scientific interests. By contrast, the recent growth of highly specialized scientific disciplines possessing knowledge of great value to private industry, the increasing dependence upon an educational establishment for skilled personnel, and the massive commitment of federal funds since World War II to the higher-education-research establishment has involved a volume of resources and a scale of organization totally different from the environment of the nineteenth century. The industrialization of the American economy in the nineteenth century focused strongly upon the development of a machine technology. The invention of new machines or machine-made products—cotton gin, reaper, thresher, cultivator, typewriter, barbed wire, revolver, sewing machine, bicycle, and later the automobile—involved the solution of problems which required mechanical skill, ingenuity and versatility but not, typically, a recourse to scientific knowledge or elaborate experimental methods. In related areas where such knowledge would have been highly relevant, e.g., in guiding metallurgical practice, the knowledge was, as we will see, virtually nonexistent. Until roughly the last third of the nineteenth century, when modern metallurgical science, involving a serious study of the structure and chemical composition of material, began, metallurgy was an area dominated by a crude empiricism of trial and error techniques. These techniques, however crude and "unscientific," were nevertheless successful in bringing about the great increases in the output of metals upon which the early stages of industrialization vitally depended. By contrast with the late twentieth century, therefore, when technical progress in many areas is thrust closely against the constraints imposed by the knowledge frontier, the growth of an industrial society in the United States made enormous strides on the basis of mechanical ingenuity and crude empiricism, and a growing mastery of metal-using techniques, but with a relatively limited use of scientific knowledge. We will return to this subject shortly; indeed, much of this volume is directly concerned with the progressive loosening of supply side constraints.

PRICE-INDUCED ADAPTATIONS

We have discussed so far the ways in which demand and supply forces affect the allocation of inventive resources. But the effect of market forces upon the broader process of technological change is much more general and pervasive than has so far been explicitly recognized.

First of all, the price mechanism is critical to the *selection* of a technology. Given the range of available productive techniques of differing factor intensities, and given also the existing prices of the factors of production, the appropriate least-cost technique can be determined. Relative price differences, therefore, provide an important explanation for observable differences in techniques employed between regions or countries. The American substitution of wood in uses where the British had employed masonry, brick, or metals, is a case in point. Furthermore, *changes* in relative factor prices will account, over time, for decisions to adopt techniques of differing factor intensities from those previously employed. Similarly, since factor prices determine the profitability of different techniques, they may be expected to be a major influence also upon the speed with which specific innovations are adopted in different countries or regions.

Secondly, relative prices of factors may influence not only the selection among existing techniques, but they may influence the *direction* of technological change as well. Under strictly competitive conditions an inventor will not be concerned with the relative factor-saving bias of a potential invention. Cost reduction will be sought in any and all directions, and whether a particular invention will have a labor-saving, resource-saving, or capital-saving bias is of no particular interest. As Salter has put it, speaking of Hicks's theory of induced inventions:

If . . . the theory implies that dearer labour stimulates the search for new knowledge aimed specifically at saving labour, then it is open to serious objections. The entrepreneur is interested in reducing costs in total, not particular costs such as labour costs or capital costs. When labour costs rise any advance that reduces total cost is welcome, and whether this is achieved by saving labour or capital is irrelevant. There is no reason to assume that attention should be concentrated on labour-saving techniques. . . .[29]

On the other hand, if there are firmly-held expectations about the *future* path of relative price changes, the pay-off function to invention will be influenced by these expectations. If, for example, businessmen infer that, in the past, there has been a historical trend, associated with a high rate of capital accumulation, for the capital-labor ratio to rise and if, in the

---

29. W. E. G. Salter, *Productivity and Technical Change* (Cambridge: Cambridge University, Department of Applied Economics, 1960), pp. 43–44.

absence of contrary evidence, they *extrapolate* this trend into the future, their expectations will be that labor costs will rise relative to the cost of capital. It will therefore pay to attempt to invent in the direction which will economize upon the factor of production whose relative price is expected to increase. Such expectations appear to have played a major role in the widely observed and much-commented-upon[30] propensity of Americans to favor *invention as well as adoption* of labor-saving machinery. It was not so much the high level of wages but rather the persistent experience of pressures on the labor market, the numerous opportunities elsewhere in a resource-abundant environment, and the high degree of labor mobility which conditioned people to expect further future increases in the cost of labor relative to other inputs. Hence a strong bias toward the development of labor-saving techniques.[31] It should be noted, however, that the motivation is perfectly general. Firmly-held expectations about the future rise in the relative price of *any* input will be expected to induce exploratory activity to economize on the use of that particular input.[32]

30. Most recently by H. J. Habakkuk, *American and British Technology in the Nineteenth Century* (New York: Cambridge University Press, 1962). See also the reports of British Commissioners in the early 1850s in Rosenberg (ed.), *op. cit.*

31. Cf. William Fellner, "Two Propositions in the Theory of Induced Innovations," *Economic Journal,* June 1961, pp. 305–308; and Lebergott, *op. cit.,* pp. 230–232. Lebergott makes the interesting point that ". . . the incentive to minimize the use of labor was emphasized for the many entrepreneurs—farmers, millers, carpenters, etc.—by the fact that they themselves had immigrated from Europe: their standard for suitable wage rates tended to be European levels. To them, especially, United States wage rates were 'high' in some absolute sense. And labor costs, having so high a visibility, were surely to be minimized." *Ibid.,* p. 231.

32. As, for example in developing the technology after 1860 which made it possible for American locomotives to utilize coal rather than cordwood fuel inputs. Fishlow points out that ". . . it was not so much the initially high price of cordwood that motivated the first research as the prospect of much higher

Finally, it must be emphasized that inventions contributed to economic growth not as a function of the timing of their invention but rather as determined by their rate of adoption and diffusion. Our earlier discussion would lead us to expect that any particular invention would vary very much in its relative attractiveness in different economic environments. In fact, relative profitability, as we will see, serves as a powerful explanatory variable in understanding the timing and the rate at which major inventions have been adopted in the past. The point is of great importance in understanding the relationship between technological change and the growth in long-term productivity. New techniques raise productivity only when, and to the extent that, they are adopted by new users. Therefore, much of the process of economic growth really centers upon the diffusion of new techniques.

future cordwood prices due to rapidly growing demand and inelastic supply." Albert Fishlow, "Productivity and Technological Change in the Railroad Sector, 1840–1910," in Brady (ed.), *op. cit.*, p. 619.

CHAPTER III

The Nineteenth Century: America as Borrower

Since an exhaustive description of the whole range of technological changes would quickly engulf the reader in a morass of tedious detail which would, in any case, add little to our general perspective or understanding, we will, for the nineteenth century, employ a different approach. When the U.S. began to industrialize in the nineteenth century, she was following a path which had been blazed earlier by Great Britain. Much of the technology which was introduced into America during this period was in fact borrowed from that country, with varying degrees of modification. With respect to the major components of industrial change—the substitution of machinery for handicraft skills, the widespread application of new power sources to industry and transportation, and the massive utilization of iron (and later, steel)—the U.S. was drawing upon a stock of innovations which had already been developed and employed in Great Britain. We will, therefore, focus first in this chapter upon this important borrowing process, with particular attention to the factors affecting the rate of diffusion of the basic inventions of the steam engine and the new ironmaking technology. In so doing, we will come to grips with some of the economic forces shaping the adoption patterns of a technology when it is transferred to a new environment. Having done this, we will then turn in the next chapter to those forces which appear to have been technologically more distinctive in the forward thrust of American production methods as they developed in the nineteenth century. Following this two-stage treatment of the nineteenth century, we will turn in Chapter V to the more complex nature of technological change in the twentieth century as it emerged out of its nineteenth-century origins. Even this chronological separation, it should be understood, is for expository convenience only, and will not—in fact cannot—be adhered to strictly. Indeed, the case of energy utilization is one where the long-term continuities are so strong that, in spite of our separate discussion of the steam engine in the nineteenth century, it will be necessary to return to that subject again at a later stage for separate treatment.

Inventions, looked upon as the outcome of an economic activity, have the peculiarly attractive property (unlike tons of steel or bottles of wine) of having to be "produced" only once. Once made, they are available for use elsewhere. The U.S. in the nineteenth century, therefore, was a major beneficiary of the technological progress which had already taken place in Great Britain. In large measure, her economic development in this period involved the transfer and exploitation of British techniques. But this does not mean that the transfer process and its internal diffusion through the American economy was either a simple or effortless one. Economic considerations, to begin with, were paramount. Even in a world of perfect, instantaneous, and free communications, with no barriers whatever to the transmission of knowledge, the export of goods or the movement of people,[1] we should not expect a smooth, uniform diffusion of new techniques. Since countries differ, sometimes drastically, in the availability of factors of production, (including, it should be noted, the age structure as well as the size of their existing stocks of capital goods)[2] techniques which are efficient (i.e., minimize costs for a given volume of output) in one environment may not be efficient in another. Therefore, between two countries as differently endowed as Britain and the U.S. in the early nineteenth century, we should expect the borrowing country to borrow in a highly selective fashion: i.e., to borrow some techniques rapidly, others more slowly, and perhaps yet others not at all. Underlying the selective nature of the transfer and diffusion, then, is an economic mechanism, based upon factor proportions and factor prices, which determined the expected profitability of different techniques in a new environment.

Such a pattern of selectivity, it is argued, would constitute rational economic behavior and would reflect differences in the expected profitability of the "menu" of techniques which are available to the borrowing country. The timing of the transfers, and therefore the length of the observed historical lags, would also be affected by a second factor related to differences in resource endowment. That is, new techniques frequently require considerable *modification* before they can function successfully in a new environment. This process of modification often involves a high order of skill and ability, which is typically underestimated or ignored. Yet the *capacity* to achieve these modifications and adaptations is critical to the successful trans-

1. Until well into the nineteenth century, the British government had laws restricting the export of certain kinds of machinery and the emigration of certain kinds of skilled labor.

2. See W.E.G. Salter, *Productivity and Technical Change* (Cambridge: Cambridge University, Department of Applied Economics, 1960).

fer of a technology—a transfer which is too frequently thought of as merely a matter of transporting a piece of hardware from one location to another.

THE STEAM ENGINE

There are, as we have seen, many possible ways of thinking about technology. At one level it may be observed as a set of principles and techniques which has become embodied in a particular collection of machines, tools, or commodities. In its concrete form, however, the technology is always more specific than the knowledge which it embodies, because it has been shaped and modified in response to a very particular set of needs, goals, or resource constraints. It is helpful in examining the acquisition of steam engine technology in the U.S. to think of it in the more general and diffuse sense as a working knowledge and capacity for applying the power of steam to perform useful work. At this stage the steam engine represented a potential; it was a power source which could be used to do many possible things: most obviously, it could turn the machinery of a mill or factory or it could propel a vehicle over land or water.

The specific uses to which this newly-acquired technology was actually put in the U.S., and the timing and the location of these applications, reflected entrepreneurial expectations about the recognized or anticipated needs of this new society insofar as these needs were expected to find expression in the market place. That is to say, entrepreneurs engaged in introducing a newly-developed foreign technology for domestic use attempted to do so in a manner best calculated to promote their future profits. In so doing they were necessarily highly sensitive to the size and structure of domestic demand, to their perception of relative costs, and to their expectations about likely future changes in these magnitudes.

Within this economic matrix, then, we need to put aside the fact that the steam engine had many unique and interesting aspects from the point of view of technological history and regard it as "merely" a new source of motive or traction power.

Motive Power. As a source of motive power the steam engine competed with water, animal power and, in some places, wind and, of course, human muscle power. The willingness to adopt the new power source depended, first of all, upon the demand for power and, second, upon the availability and the cost of alternative forms of power. These considerations explain why, within the U.S., steam power for motive purposes was only slowly adopted. Industry in the early nineteenth century was heavily concentrated in New England. Although the demand for power was great and the capacity to produce steam engines was certainly well-established by the 1830s, an excellent and cheaper substitute in the form of water power was provided along the fall line by the numerous, fast-flowing rivers and streams of New England. The growing reliance upon steam power was, in fact, closely connected with the westward movement of population and industry into a geographic region which offered fewer sources of water power and where, as a result, the economic significance of steam power was greater

It is important to note, then, that mechanization in the U.S. did not initially involve any massive shift to new power sources. U.S. Census reports indicate that American manufacturing relied upon water as its main source of power until well into the second half of the nineteenth century. Indeed, as late as 1869 steam power accounted for barely over one-half of primary-power capacity in manufacturing—51.8 percent as compared to 48.2 percent for water.[3] In general, it may be said that steam power tended to be adopted in locations where water power sources were scarce and where fuel sources were either abundant or cheaply transportable. One important consequence of improvements in transportation, therefore, was the expansion of the area within which steam power could be profitably employed.[4]

It is quite clear that the relatively slow adoption of the stationary steam engine even in the second third of the nineteenth century was *not* due to an inability of Americans to manufacture steam engines. In fact, data collected in the late 1830s demonstrate that by 1838 there were some 250 or so steam engine builders, mostly very small scale businesses, widely scattered throughout the U.S. A government report on steam engines in the U.S. (known to be somewhat incomplete) estimated that there were more than 1,800 stationary steam engines in operation in 1838.[5] American mechanical skills by this date were

3. Allen H. Fenichel, "Growth and Diffusion of Power in Manufacturing, 1839–1919," in Brady (ed.), *Output, Employment and Productivity in the United States after 1800, op. cit.*, Appendix B. For 1879 the proportions were: steam power 64.1% and water power 35.9%. In 1889 steam power had risen to 78.4% and water power had declined to 21.5%. Fenichel also reports that "steam-power capacity grew from 36,100 horsepower in 1839 to 1,216,000 horse-power in 1869 to 13,840,000 horsepower in 1919; and water-power capacity grew from 1,130,000 to 1,765,000 horsepower between 1869 and 1919." *Ibid.*, p. 444.

4. The impact of transportation improvements is, of course, a complex issue. Reductions in transport costs also expand the markets available to commodities which are produced by water power, and may thereby retard the introduction of steam power elsewhere.

5. U.S. Congress, House, *Report on the Steam Engines in the United States*, H. Doc. No. 21, 25th Congress, 3d Session, 1839, p. 376. The data in this report have recently been exploited by Peter Temin, "Steam and Waterpower in the Early Nineteenth Century," *Journal of Economic History*, June 1966, pp. 187–205. See also Carroll Pursell, Jr., *Early Stationary Steam Engines in America* (Washington, D.C.: Smithsonian Institute, 1969). It is possible that, at least in the earlier years, the oft-cited greater reliability of steam power over water power

obviously well-developed, and there was no slavish reliance upon or imitation of British models and techniques. This is most apparent in the American use of the high pressure steam engine. Although the high pressure steam engine had been developed simultaneously by Richard Trevithick in Great Britain and Oliver Evans in the U.S. in the opening years of the nineteenth century, British practice subsequently strongly favored the low pressure stationary engine while Americans overwhelmingly adopted the high-pressure stationary engine.[6] On the other hand, the American preference for water power over steam, especially in New England, was a consequence of the abundant supplies of running water, which Americans exploited by the construction of the cheaper forms of water wheels. These wheels were, in a strictly engineering sense, highly inefficient. However, they were preferred to wheels which utilized a higher proportion of the available water power, but which involved a larger initial capital expenditure.[7] The situation changed after 1840 as the limited number of more attractive water sites even in New England was exhausted and the demand for power continued to grow rapidly. Nevertheless, although the efficiency (as measured, for example, in coal requirements per unit of horse power) of the steam engine

was not so decisive as is commonly supposed. Although the supply of water power was likely to be erratic due to seasonal variations resulting from drought, frost, or flood, the early steam engines were also subject to frequent breakdowns and extensive maintenance requirements which may not have been readily catered to.

6. Temin, *op. cit.*, pp. 188–189. High pressure steam engines were cheaper to construct than low pressure engines but were profligate in their utilization of fuel. These characteristics made such engines attractive in the resource-abundant environment of the U.S. where it was worthwhile, in effect, to "trade off" relative large amounts of natural resource inputs for a reduction in fixed capital costs.

7. Victor S. Clark, *History of Manufactures in the United States*, 3 vols. (New York: Carnegie Institution, 1929), 1: 406.

improved and its cost declined, there were also major improvements in the utilization of water power. This particularly took the form, after 1840, of the water turbine, an important invention of French origin.[8] The decisive significance of geography in influencing the selection of technology is indicated by the fact that, as late as 1869, by which time steam had just surpassed water on a national basis as a source of power, less than 30 percent of the power employed in New England manufacturing establishments was derived from steam.[9] New England industry for long remained heavily concentrated in communities which offered superior access to water power—Lowell, Lawrence, Hadley Falls, Holyoke, Chicopee, Springfield, Waterbury, Manchester.[10]

Tractive Power. Although the availability of a good substitute slowed the pace at which the stationary steam engine was acquired in the U.S., the situation was vastly different in the application of steam power to transportation. The U.S. comprised a land area of continental proportions.[11] So long as population

8. *Ibid.*, pp. 406–408. France's contribution to improving the technology of hydraulic engines, especially as represented by the path-breaking work of Poncelet and Fourneyron, should be seen against the background of her relative scarcity of coal resources.

9. Fenichel, *op. cit.*, p. 456.

10. An American who had visited the industrial cities of England in 1825 pointed emphatically to the locational consequences of heavy American reliance upon water power: "The manufacturing operations in the United States are all carried on in little hamlets, which often appear to spring up in the bosom of some forest, gathered around the water fall that serves to turn the mill wheel. These villages are scattered over a vast extent of country, from Indiana to the Atlantic, and from Maine to North Carolina, instead of being collected together, as they are in England, in great manufacturing districts. A stranger, therefore, in travelling through the United States, can form but an imperfect estimate of the extent of manufacturing operations carried on therein." Zachariah Allen, *The Science of Mechanics* (Providence, R.I.: 1829), p. 352.

11. At least it did after the Louisiana Purchase in 1803. An important motive in consummating that substantial real estate transaction was the fact that the

was confined to a relatively narrow strip of land east of the Appalachians, the Atlantic Ocean and its bays, sounds and tidal rivers offered a reasonably adequate basis for the movement of goods. But the exploitation of the trans-Appalachian West was dependent upon innovations which would liberate commerce from the prohibitively high cost of land transport and the upstream haulage of goods. It is perhaps not too much to say that the major economic consequence of the acquisition of the steam engine in the New World before the Civil War lay in its application to new forms of transport—the steamboat and later the railroad—which (together with the canal) provided a network for the cheap movement of goods, especially bulky agricultural products. The contrast between the relatively slow adoption of the stationary steam engine and the rapid exploitation of the steam engine for transport purposes is, in fact, highly instructive. It is an excellent demonstration of the manner in which social needs, as expressed in the marketplace, and as they influenced business profit expectations, shaped and directed the pattern of innovative activity. For within the context of the antebellum American economy the abundance of water power in the East and the huge size of the land area awaiting exploitation in the West shifted the attention of inventors and entrepreneurs away from the use of the steam engine as a stationary power source and into its rapid exploitation as a device for the conquest of space.

As a source of tractive power, the steam engine in the early nineteenth century had many substitutes—animals and animal-drawn devices, running water (down which keelboats and flat-

only feasible route for the produce of the Mississippi Valley at the time lay down river by way of New Orleans. It is interesting to note that Robert Fulton's business partner was none other than Robert Livingston, Thomas Jefferson's minister to France, who had earlier negotiated the Louisiana Purchase.

boats could be cheaply floated), and sailing vessels. But the geography—the scale and disposition of resources—was such that the vast area of the trans-Appalachian West could not be exploited without major reductions in transport costs from some new source. This was clearly perceived by a series of fertile and inventive minds—Oliver Evans, John Fitch, Robert Fulton, James Ramsey, and John Stevens—who were aware of the great lag in the reduction of overland transport costs behind those of water, and for whom the steam engine represented, above all, a new and much-cheapened form of transportation. If America led the world in the development and exploitation of the steamboat by the second quarter of the nineteenth century, it was largely because the economic pay-off to this innovation was correctly perceived to be very great in a large, undeveloped country, rich in natural resources and with a vast system of natural internal waterways. By contrast with Great Britain and Western Europe, which were comparatively well served by coastal waterways and canals, the steamboat in the immense Mississippi basin offered a form of transportation far superior at the time to the available alternatives. Although the early experiments with the steamboat were, inevitably, conducted on eastern waterways, men like Fitch, Evans, and Fulton clearly understood that the great utility of the steamboat would be on the western rivers.[12] The steamboat was rapidly

12. After the successful maiden voyage of the *Clermont*, the *American Citizen*, a New York newspaper, wrote of "Mr. Fulton's ingenious Steam Boat, invented with a view to the navigation of the Mississippi from New Orleans upwards. . . ." Fulton himself stated, at the same time, that the steamboat ". . . will give a cheap and quick conveyance to the merchandise on the Mississippi, Missouri, and other great rivers, which are now laying open their treasures to the enterprise of our countrymen." As quoted in Louis Hunter, *Steamboats on the Western Rivers* (Cambridge, Mass.: Harvard University Press, 1949), p. 8.

introduced into the Mississippi basin after Robert Fulton's successful demonstration on the Hudson River with the *Clermont* in 1807. Four years later the *New Orleans* negotiated the trip from Pittsburgh to the city whose name it bore. In 1815 the *Enterprise* completed the much more difficult—and economically more significant—trip upriver. From this point on, the steamboat quickly achieved great success on western rivers and, in this form, the steam engine dominated the economic life of the Mississippi Valley for a generation (see Table 2).

Even the twelve-fold increase in tonnage between 1820 and 1860 drastically understates the growth in transport services provided by the steamboat because of major increases in speed and in cargo capacity in relation to measured tonnage. Because of such improvements Hunter concludes that "... the facilities of steamboat transportation on the western rivers during a period of forty years multiplied not twelvefold but more than one hundred and twentyfold."[13]

The extent to which American exploitation of steam was dominated by the steamboat before 1840 may be simply stated. According to the *Report on Steam Engines,* almost 60 percent of all power generated by steam in 1838 was accounted for by steamboat engines.[14]

If one asks precisely what it was which was "acquired" from the Old World by the Americans who created this vast inland fleet, the answer is by no means obvious. Certainly there was the steam engine itself, and the knowledge of its operating

13. *Ibid.,* p. 34.
14. *Report on Steam Engines, op. cit.,* p. 10. The figures, mostly reported but partly estimated, were:

Steamboats —	57,019	horse power
Railroads —	6,980	
Others —	36,319	
Total	100,318	horse power

Table 2

Steamboats Operating on the Western Rivers
1817–1860

Year	Number	Tonnage
1817	17	3,290
1820	69	13,890
1823	75	12,501
1825	73	9,992
1830	187	29,481
1836	381	57,090
1840	536	83,592
1845	557	98,246
1850	740	141,834
1855	727	173,068
1860	735	162,735

Source: Hunter, *op. cit.*, p. 33. Reprinted by permission of Harvard University Press.

principles as well as techniques of construction. Some of the steam engines installed in the first steamboats were imported from Great Britain—indeed, Fulton himself had installed a Boulton and Watt steam engine in the Clermont. But America quickly acquired the skills to provide her own engines, and produced them to her own design in large quantities in the main centers of steamboat construction—Pittsburgh, Cincinnati, and Louisville.[15]

Basically the steamboat at the time of its inception was a clumsy merger of the steam engine with an ordinary ocean-going vessel. With its deep and rounded hulls, projecting keel, heavy frame, and low-profile superstructure of a sailing vessel, it was remarkably ill-adapted to the shallow-water navigation of inland rivers. The transformation of the basic design of the steamboat occurred very quickly, and yet it is difficult to iden-

15. Hunter, *op. cit.*, pp. 122–123.

tify this transformation with specific inventions. Rather, the steamboat underwent a series of innumerable, indeed continuous, changes in structural design and proportions which made of it the maneuverable, flat-bottom, shallow draft, high superstructured vessel which it had to be to negotiate western rivers with substantial cargoes.[16] The steamboats were powered by high pressure engines whose wastefulness in fuel consumption as compared with low pressure engines was more than offset by low cost of construction and repair and relative compactness. Since cordwood was abundant and cheap along the banks of the Ohio and Mississippi Rivers, economy of fuel consumption was of less consequence than in the East, where there was a greater preference for the low pressure engine.[17]

The story of the steamboat, then, is a story of continuous modification and adaptation of a general concept—the possibility of propelling a large cargo vessel by means of a steam engine —to the highly specific characteristics of a particular environment. The end-product of this adaptiveness—one might even say "evolution"—was a unique instrument ideally suited to a particular set of economic and geographic circumstances.[18]

16. The story of this transformation is beautifully told in Hunter, *op. cit.*, chap. 2.

17. *Ibid.*, pp. 130, 133.

18. Application of steam power to vessels was not, of course, confined to western rivers. Indeed, as measured in absolute tonnage, western steamboats never accounted for as much as half of the national tonnage (Hunter, *op. cit.*, p. 33). However, steam power long continued to be dominated by sailing vessels in the lake trade, coastal trade, and international trade. For long distance traffic the space required by steam vessels for bulky machinery and fuel supplies was a major deterrent, and the abundance of timber in the U.S. reduced the initial capital costs of wooden sailing vessels to levels which enabled them to compete successfully for many years with the new technology of iron-hulled, propeller-driven steamships. American leadership in the application of steam power to river traffic was in no way matched by its ocean-going merchant marine, which in fact lagged seriously behind European maritime progress.

Although space considerations preclude any detailed treatment of the acquisition of railroad technology, a few remarks are in order.[19] In contrast to the steamboat where the U.S. asserted an early leadership, the U.S. relied much more heavily upon British leadership and prior development in the case of railroads.

The U.S. was much more directly dependent upon Britain in the application of the steam engine to land transport than it had been in the case of the steamboat. Britain was clearly the pioneer and major innovator in the case of the railroad, and America the follower. Yet it is notable how quickly the student acquired a competence and became independent, at least with respect to rolling stock. Only a limited number of locomotives were imported from Britain even in the earliest years. In the early 1830s locomotives began to be built in foundries, machine shops, and textile machinery plants, and in Philadelphia the

19. The contribution of the railroad to the growth of the American economy in the nineteenth century has been subjected to a searching reexamination in recent years. See the seminal work of Robert Fogel, *Railroads and American Economic Growth* (Baltimore, Md.: Johns Hopkins Press, 1964), and Albert Fishlow, *American Railroads and the Transformation of the Ante-Bellum Economy* (Cambridge, Mass.: Harvard University Press, 1965). Fogel argues that the contribution of the railroads to American economic growth in the nineteenth century has been exaggerated in the works of earlier historians. Although an efficient system of internal transportation was essential to American development, the railroads themselves were not indispensable because reasonable alternative modes of transport were available. Yet, although Fogel's book deals with the role of the railroad in American economic growth, his central concern is to attack what he calls the "Axiom of Indispensability." "The most important implication of this study is that no single innovation was vital for economic growth during the nineteenth century. Certainly if any innovation had title to such distinction it was the railroad. Yet, despite its dramatically rapid and massive growth over a period of a half century, despite its eventual ubiquity in inland transportation, despite its devouring appetite for capital, despite its power to determine the outcome of commercial (and sometimes political) competition, the railroad did not make an overwhelming contribution to the production potential of the economy." Fogel, *op. cit.*, pp. 234-235.

specialized Baldwin locomotive works was established in 1832 and the Norris firm two years later. Only 117 of the 450 locomotives in the U.S. at the end of 1839 had been imported from England, and most of these imports had occurred before 1836.[20]

The situation was very different with respect to rails, where Britain's more advanced iron making plants and rolling mills conferred a price advantage on British rail makers great enough to overcome the additional costs of ocean shipping, commissions, etc. American railroads remained heavily dependent upon imports of British rails for many years. During the western railway construction boom from 1849 to 1854, 80 percent of American railway iron requirements were met by imports.[21] American ironmaking capacity expanded thereafter (with some initial emphasis on rerolling), in no small measure due to the insistent demands of the railroads. Although America supplied most of her own rails by the late 1850s, British imports continued to be a significant proportion of the total during peak construction years such as the late 1860s, early 1870s and, to a lesser extent, early 1880s.[22]

In spite of this reliance upon British experience and supplies, American railroads showed a high degree of responsiveness to unique aspects of the American scene, and American engineers and builders demonstrated an imaginative capacity to modify and adapt the foreign model in significant ways. The relative cheapness of wood to iron in the U.S. led to extensive substitu-

20. Fishlow, *op. cit.*, p. 149. Fishlow also reports that "for other rolling stock there is no evidence of reliance upon foreign products."

21. Fishlow, *op. cit.*, pp. 137–138.

22. Peter Temin, *Iron and Steel in Nineteenth-Century America*, (Cambridge, Mass.: M.I.T. Press, 1964), Appendix C, Table C6. By the late 1870s the rails were mostly steel rails, which had a much longer useful life expectancy than those made of iron.

tion of wood in uses where the British had employed iron. In numerous ways capital outlays in the early years were reduced by building the roads to specifications which British engineers would have considered unacceptable: steep gradients and sharp curvatures were tolerated, and the construction of tunnels was avoided whenever possible.[23] One of the main results of such construction was to raise fuel input requirements of railroad operation. Given the general abundance of fuel and relative scarcity of capital, however, such a substitution of (cheap) natural resource inputs for (expensive) capital inputs was eminently "rational." The Americans also reduced initial construction costs by purchasing low-quality British rails.[24]

Moreover, as the relative prices of inputs altered, so did railroad practice. For example, up until the Civil War American locomotives were almost totally committed to wood as a fuel.

Within a score of years thereafter, a transformation so rapid had occurred that twenty times more coal than wood was being consumed annually, and more than a fourth of bituminous coal output was regularly absorbed by the railway sector. The underlying mechanism is almost a text book illustration of substitution in response to changing relative prices. To begin with, eastern railroads with large coal deposits

23. One of the serious problems in adapting the locomotive to the American scene was to design engines which would perform effectively on the short curves prevalent on American railroads. Baldwin's solution was the flexible beam truck, for which he received a patent in 1842. *History of the Baldwin Locomotive Works 1832–1913*, no author, no date, pp. 30–34.

24. "In 1867 Abram Hewitt said that 'In the Welsh iron works . . . it was humiliating to find that the vilest trash which could be dignified by the name of iron went universally by the name of the American rail.' Though the Welsh ironmasters greatly preferred to turn out good work, their American customers had the 'stupidity and reckless extravagance' to insist on buying at the lowest price, irrespective of quality. (British railways at that time usually bought under a guarantee of seven years' life for which they paid a substantial premium.)" J. C. Carr and W. Taplin, *History of the British Steel Industry*, (Oxford: Basil Blackwell, 1962), p. 60 n. 3.

along their lines, and hence both low coal prices and elastic supply, invested in research necessary to eliminate the troublesome technical problems that had limited the development of coal-burning locomotives. Once successful, the eastern railroads penalized by high wood prices and the western railroads favored by low coal prices led the parade to mineral fuel.[25]

Finally, we may note that the Russians sought out an American engineer to supervise the construction of a railway from St. Petersburg to Moscow as early as the 1840s. Such a selection, somewhat startling at first glance, may have reflected a shrewd awareness that Russian and American conditions closely resembled one another, and that an American engineer would be more likely than an English one to modify the new railroad technology in accordance with the peculiar needs of the Russian environment.[26]

METALLURGY

Improvements in metallurgy were fundamental to industrialization. The new machines, the remarkable feats of construction and civil engineering, and the revolution in transport are difficult to conceive of without large quantities of cheap iron (and later, steel). In examining this transfer, we are confronted

25. Albert Fishlow, "Productivity and Technological Change in the Railroad Sector, 1840–1910," in Brady (ed.), *op. cit.*, p. 619.

26. The engineer was Major George Washington Whistler, father of the artist. Whistler also constructed locomotives and their equipment in a factory which had been established for that purpose. See Albert Parry, *Whistler's Father* (Indianapolis, Ind.: Bobbs-Merrill Company, 1939). "How smart this foreign gentleman," the awed muzhiks are reported to have exclaimed, "who has harnessed the samovar and made it run." *Ibid.*, p. xvi.

The Baldwin Locomotive Works in Philadelphia filled orders for large numbers of locomotives for Russian railways in the 1870s and 1890s. *History of the Baldwin Locomotive Works, op. cit.*, pp. 67–68, 73, 85.

with the intriguing fact that, unlike the rapid imitation or even leadership which the U.S. quickly demonstrated with respect to the uses of the steam engine, the country lagged several decades behind the best practice techniques of the British iron industry It is a striking fact that, whereas the mechanical technology of the steam engine fairly leaped across the barrier of the Atlantic Ocean, changes in metallurgical technology moved at a pace which seemed glacial by comparison.

This statement requires qualification. The lag in the transfer of the new iron technology was much smaller at the stage of refining the pig iron into wrought iron (the complex of innovations involving puddling with the use of mineral fuel and the shaping of the wrought iron by rolling instead of hammering) than at the stage of smelting of the iron ore in the blast furnace.[27]

The introduction of mineral fuel into the blast furnace in England was the outcome of a protracted search for a cheap substitute for wood fuel going back to the early seventeenth century. While we cannot be detained here by this fascinating piece of technological history, it should at least be pointed out that very little is known of the diffusion of Darby's coke-smelting process after his initial success in 1709.[28] The shift from charcoal

27. See Temin, *op. cit.*, chaps. 1 and 5. It is interesting to note that, on the European continent as well, mineral fuel was introduced more rapidly at the refining than at the smelting stage. Landes points out: "In contrast to Britain, where puddling came more than half a century after coke smelting, the continental countries learned to refine with coal first. This is the normal sequence technologically: the fuel and ore economies are greater in refining; the absence of direct contact between fuel and metal excludes some of the most serious difficulties associated with the chemical composition of the materials employed; and the initial cost of the shift to coal in refining is much less than in smelting." David Landes, *The Unbound Prometheus* (Cambridge: Cambridge University Press, 1969), pp. 175–176.

28. T. S. Ashton, *Iron and Steel in the Industrial Revolution* (Manchester: Manchester University Press, 1924), chap. 2 (reprinted in 1963 with a valuable bibliographical note by W. H. Chaloner); M. W. Flinn, "Abraham Darby and the coke-smelting process," *Economica*, February 1959, pp. 54–59.

to coke in the blast furnace was accelerated in the second half of the eighteenth century and was virtually completed by 1800.[29]

The situation in the U.S. stood in striking contrast to this. As late as 1840 almost 100 percent of all pig iron produced in the U.S. was still made with charcoal, and even as late as 1860 only a scant 13 percent of American pig iron was being smelted with the "modern" fuel—coke.[30]

In coming to grips with the American lag in the adoption of the new iron technology, we must recognize that metallurgy differs from more purely mechanical technology in some important ways. Most important for present purposes is the fact that metallurgical processes are intimately enmeshed with the physical environment, linked up with qualities of the natural resource inputs—qualities which simply were not understood in any serious scientific sense until the latter part of the nineteenth century. Metallurgy in the period under review was still essentially an activity relying upon crude empiricism. Variations in resource inputs affected the success of the productive process in ways which could be observed experimentally but not understood or predicted. Resource inputs which were best suited could be found by a trial-and-error process much as nineteenth-century frontier farmers might experiment with a variety of wheat seeds in a new climate until they found the kinds which "worked best."[31] Thus, although a long list of English-

29. Ashton states: "Already in 1788 there were 59 coke furnaces in blast, as against 26 charcoal furnaces, but by 1806 the coke furnaces numbered 162, and only 11 charcoal furnaces were to be found in the whole of Great Britain." Ashton, op. cit., p. 99.

30. Temin, op. cit., p. 82 and Appendix C, Table C3.

31. This was true also in other spheres where important qualities of natural resource inputs were not understood. The results which could nevertheless be achieved by careful observation and systematic empiricism, are well illustrated in the following quotation: "When John Smeaton was commissioned to build the third Eddystone lighthouse, he realized the importance of using a strongly

men had attempted—unsuccessfully—to introduce mineral fuel into the blast furnace, Abraham Darby succeeded where others had failed partly because of the simple geological fact that the coal which was found conveniently near the surface at Coalbrookdale happened to be of a chemical composition peculiarly appropriate for smelting.[32] Similarly, Bessemer's success in the mid-nineteenth century had been conditioned by the fact that he used imported Swedish iron in his experiments —iron which, as it happened, was singularly free of phosphorus, although Bessemer was not aware of this fact. Indeed, the acute distress of British ironmakers who attempted, unsuccessfully, to reproduce Bessemer's method with British ores containing substantial amounts of phosphorus was a major event leading to the emergence of the modern science of metallurgy.[33]

hydraulic lime to join the masonry, in addition to dove-tailing and dowelling the stones together. He collected samples of lime from many parts of the country, tested them for strength, and submitted them to chemical analysis. He thus discovered that this property of setting under water was always found in a lime made from a limestone that contained an appreciable proportion of clay. This discovery formed the basis of a number of 'natural' and 'artificial' cements. The natural cements were made from minerals in which calcareous and argillaceous constituents were present in roughly suitable proportions to make, when calcined and finely ground, an 'eminently hydraulic' lime. The best known of these was the so-called Roman cement, which was supposed to make mortar or concrete as hard as the best specimens surviving from the Roman occupation. . . . The artificial cements were made by mixing together chalk or limestone and clay or mud in proportions that had to be empirically determined, because the chemical reactions involved in the setting and hardening of cement were then unknown; they are in fact highly complicated. . . ." S. B. Hamilton, "Building and Civil Engineering Construction," in Singer et al. (ed.), *A History of Technology, op. cit.*, 4: 447–448.

32. Ashton, *op. cit.*, pp. 33–34.

33. Only later was it established that the chemical composition of the iron exerted a decisive effect upon the quality of the final product. Indeed, iron containing more than 0.1 percent phosphorus was unsuitable for the original (acid) Bessemer process. The introduction of the basic lining by the British chemists, Gilchrist and Thomas, in the late 1870s, made it possible to use phosphoric ores. The basic Bessemer process, however, in turn *required*

It is the combination of (1) this critical role of particular qualities of resource inputs as they determined their economic usefulness with (2) the specific locational matrix in which these resources were embedded, which accounted for the large American lag in the acquisition of the new British iron technology. The economic importance of locational factors is seen in the rapid shift of the British iron industry to the coal fields of the Midlands, Yorkshire and Derbyshire, and South Wales, as coal was substituted for charcoal. Since it required, with the early nineteenth-century ironmaking technology, several times as much coal as iron ore to produce a ton of iron, proximity to coal became a dominant economic consideration.[34]

In the first decades of the nineteenth century when it still employed the charcoal technology, the blast furnaces of the U.S. were spread out along the eastern seaboard. Pig iron production, requiring large amounts of wood fuel, was widely diffused geographically—as it had to be. The increasing demand for iron was met essentially by increasing the number of charcoal blast furnaces. The new British blast furnace technology was not adopted because bituminous coal was required for coking purposes, and the known deposits of such coal suffered from two deficiencies: (1) they contained substantial amounts of sulfur, which made for the production of poor quality pig iron, and (2) they were located west of the

phosphoric iron and could not be used unless the iron contained *more* than 1.5 percent phosphorus. Since the United States contains only very limited amounts of ores which were suitable for exploitation by the basic Bessemer process, the technique was never widely employed in this country.

34. See Walter Isard, "Some Locational Factors in the Iron and Steel Industry since the Early Nineteenth Century," *Journal of Political Economy*, June 1948, pp. 203–217.

Allegheny Mountains, far from the country's population centers.[35]

America *did*, however, possess some very rich coal deposits in eastern Pennsylvania. But this was anthracite coal, a coal containing neither gas nor sulfur. Although the absence of sulfur meant that it could be used to produce high quality pig iron, the absence of gas made ignition much more difficult and meant that it could not be used employing the blast furnace technology developed by the British in the eighteenth century.[36]

This situation was altered by the development in England of the hot blast, an innovation which, by preheating the blast before entering the furnace, and later by employing waste gases from the furnace itself, permitted substantial fuel economies.[37] *Here we observe virtually no lag at all in the transfer of the technique from Britain to the U.S.* The method was first employed in England in 1828 and by 1834 it was successfully introduced into a blast furnace in New Jersey.[38] But the important point for present purposes is that, during the 1830s a Welshman, David Thomas, discovered that the use of the hot blast made it possible to introduce anthracite as a fuel into the blast furnace. Thomas actually came to the U.S. where he constructed the first successful anthracite blast furnace in 1839. From that point on, the expansion of pig iron output employing anthracite proceeded rapidly.

35. In this age of the jet airplane and high-speed turnpike travel it takes perhaps a stretch of the imagination to recall that, until the construction of the railroads in the 1850s, the Alleghenies constituted an almost impenetrable barrier to the movement of bulky freight between Pittsburgh and Philadelphia.

36. The greater resistance of anthracite to combustion may also have been responsible for the delay in the introduction of the important practice of "hard driving" into the U.S. See Temin, *op. cit.*, pp. 157–163.

37. *Ibid.*, pp. 57–62.

38. *Ibid.*, pp. 57–59.

Thus, when the U.S. finally introduced a mineral fuel into the blast furnace, it was based upon a newly-developed British technique. This technique was rapidly adopted because it permitted the exploitation of a resource which was highly abundant and readily accessible to America's main population centers. Anthracite furnaces accounted for one half of pig iron output in 1856.[39]

The eventual adoption of the earlier coke smelting technology came only in the post-Civil War years. In the late 1850s the proportion of pig iron smelted with coke still did not exceed 10 percent of total output. By 1870 this figure was 31 percent, by 1880, 45 percent, by 1890, 69 percent and, in the first years of the twentieth century the proportion rose to over 90 percent.[40] The major breakthrough was linked, again, to the subtle interplay between the specific resource requirements of a particular technology and the sequence in which the resource base was gradually uncovered. [41] Along with the westward movement of population and the more intensive exploration of the trans-Appalachian west, came the discovery of the high-quality coking coal in the Connellsville region of Pennsylvania. The first blast furnace designed specifically for the exploitation of Connellsville coke was built in Pittsburgh in 1859. The physical structure of the coal and the absence of sulfur made it possible to produce pig iron of high quality. This, together with the development of a low-cost transportation network and further technical developments favorable to coke, assured the eventual domination of this fuel in the blast furnace. The dominance of anthracite in 1860, then, when it accounted for over one half

39. *Ibid.*, Appendix C, Table C3.
40. *Loc. cit.*
41. In Germany there was a similar delay due to the comparatively late discovery of the richness of the coal deposits of the Ruhr.

of U.S. pig iron production, proved to be very short-lived.

In the years after the Civil War the iron industry was rapidly transformed into an iron and steel industry. Until that period the cost of steel had been so high that only a minute fraction of pig iron output was eventually refined into steel. The introduction of the Bessemer process, however, led to a spectacular growth in steel output during the 1870s and 1880s. Total steel production rose from less than 70,000 gross tons in 1870 to 1,247,000 tons in 1880; 4,277,000 tons in 1890; 10,188,000 tons in 1900; and 26,095,000 tons in 1910.[42] But the dominance of the Bessemer process was, like that of anthracite in the blast furnace, also relatively short-lived. From the second half of the 1870s until 1890 the Bessemer process accounted in each year for at least 85 percent of the total output of steel. Bessemer steel was peculiarly well suited for making high quality rails but less suited for other higher quality steel products. During the years of its supremacy a high proportion of Bessemer steel output was devoted to making rails, and the relative importance of this process began to decline in the last decade of the nineteenth century after the demand for rails had passed its peak. By 1910 the Bessemer process was producing only 36 percent of steel output, by which time the primacy of the open hearth process had been firmly established. The open hearth process, although it was not widely used until the late 1880s, grew rapidly in the 1890s and the first decade of the twentieth century. By 1910 it was producing 63 percent of total steel output. Although it produced a superior steel as compared to the Bessemer process,

42. Temin, *op. cit.,* Table C4. In addition to the major technical innovations in the steel industry in the decades after the Civil War, important improvements in productivity were derived from reorganization and rearrangement of plants in such ways as to minimize the necessity for the reheating of materials and to make possible a greater exploitation of by-products.

the overwhelming advantage of the basic open hearth process was its ability to utilize a wide spectrum of the abundant phosphoric ores of the United States which could not be utilized by the Bessemer process.[43]

We have stressed the roles of selectivity and modification in the transfer process, emphasizing how qualitative as well as quantitative differences in resource endowments have affected the rate and the sequence of the transfer of technology. Some further observations on this subject seem in order.

First of all, the recipient of these transfers was a nation whose level of mechanical competence and technical skills (aside from its slave population) was already very high. The fact of the matter is that it required considerable technical expertise to borrow and exploit a foreign industrial technology. This should hardly be a surprising proposition, but it seems to be worth repeating in view of the vast number of foreign aid and economic assistance programs in the years since the Second World War which have come to grief because of the absence of the appropriate skills in the receiving country. The *selection* of a technology as appropriate in a particular context, and its *adaptation* and *modification* in order to enable it to function efficiently in an environment different from the one in which it originated, are activities which typically require a very high degree of technological sophistication. Although it is difficult to

43. Temin, *op. cit.*, chap. 6. Bessemer steel tended to become brittle and was subject to an increasing frequency of breakages with age, even though it appeared to be qualitatively equal to open hearth steel when it was first produced. Although the causes of this misbehavior were hotly debated by scientists and engineers, the real reason was not correctly apprehended in the nineteenth century. Only later was it established that the true culprit was a small quantity of nitrogen which dissolved into the iron as air was blown through the molten iron in the Bessemer converter. Open hearth steel, since it was produced by an entirely different principle, did not suffer from this defect.

find data which measure directly the technical competence of a population,[44] it is interesting to recall, as we noted previously, that the U.S. compared very favorably with Western Europe as early as 1830 in certain crude measures of enrollment for formal education. Although the manner in which a society acquires and diffuses technical skills is still only very imperfectly understood, and although formal education is certainly only a part of that process, it is worth noting that there is a close correlation in the early nineteenth century between such indexes of educational attainment and the speed with which individual countries were able to adopt and modify Britain's new industrial technology.[45]

Second, our whole conception of the way in which the new technology replaces the old requires drastic modification. This is particularly important because our notions concerning both the economic and social consequences of technical change are often based on an exaggerated sense of the pace at which the new techniques replaced the old. Our understanding of the nature and the pace of historical change can be substantially improved by more detailed, quantitative knowledge of the displacement of one set of techniques by another. We have already

44. For some evidence on the supply of skilled labor in the U.S. in the 1820s, see Nathan Rosenberg, "Anglo-American Wage Differences in the 1820s," *Journal of Economic History*, June 1967, pp. 221–229.

45. Easterlin, "A Note on the Evidence of History," *op. cit.* The qualifications in the text seem important. Not all education is equally conducive to technological innovation; indeed, it may be plausibly argued that certain kinds of education have probably retarded this process. Moreover, Britain herself (see Table 1 above) did not rank terribly high in the first half of the nineteenth century in a ranking of countries by percentage of the total population enrolled in school. Yet it was Britain which *initiated* the new technology—a technology which was, moreover, rapidly diffused within that country. Acquisition of mechanical skills was, to a very large degree, an on-the-job process. The precise role of the sort of skills which are acquired through formal education is still not clearly understood.

seen the stubborn persistence of water power in the face of steam. In absolute terms the amount of power generated by water in New England continued to increase right into the twentieth century. Similarly, in 1800, by which time Watt's patents had all expired, Newcomen engines were not only still being used but, due to their low construction and maintenance costs and long life expectancy, still continuing to be *built*.[46] Although the primitive flatboat would seem to have been no match for the Mississippi steamer, flatboat arrivals at New Orleans reached their all-time high in 1846–47, at an absolute level nearly five times as great as that of 1814.[47] For, although the steamboat had decisive economic advantages in the upstream traffic, its advantages in travelling downstream were, not surprisingly, not nearly so great. By 1860 the introduction of the steamboat had resulted in a reduction of downstream transportation costs by a factor of between 3 and 4 but it had reduced upstream transportation costs by a factor of 10. Finally, the absolute output of pig iron by use of charcoal reached its peak as late as 1890, several decades after the mineral fuel technology had been introduced.

The new technology, therefore, usually asserted its advantages over the old only slowly. Partly this is because the new technique has many "bugs" at first which need to be eliminated; partly because the capital goods sector takes time to learn to produce the new machine efficiently, and the diffusion of the new technology is closely linked to the gradual decline in price which is associated with this learning process; partly

46. H. W. Dickinson, *A Short History of the Steam Engine* (Cambridge: Cambridge University Press, 1939), p. 90. Their use continued primarily near coal pits where their wastefulness of coal was less important. Some Newcomen engines even used slag coal.
47. Hunter, *op. cit.*, p. 55.

because there is another learning process in the efficient *utilization* of the capital good after it has been produced and installed; partly because improvements continue to be made in the *old* technique, as was the case with the water turbine long after the development of Watt's steam engine, and the major improvements in sailboat design after the introduction of the ocean steamer;[48] partly because the geographic distribution of resources frequently gives specific localities transport, power, or other cost advantages even with the old technology; partly because important qualitative variations in resource inputs are imperfectly understood; and partly because the process of modification to local conditions is often, as we have seen, a very time-consuming one.

48. Although total U.S. tonnage of sailing vessels peaked in 1861, steam tonnage did not exceed sail tonnage until 1893. *Historical Statistics of the United States, op. cit.*, pp. 444–445. In Britain, sailing tonnage peaked in 1865 but was not exceeded by steam tonnage until 1883. B. R. Mitchell, *Abstract of British Historical Statistics* (Cambridge: Cambridge University Press, 1962), p. 218. Of course it must be remembered that a ton of steamship did far more work than a ton of sailboat. The point is that there was no Schumpeterian "gale of creative destruction." For an interesting appraisal of Schumpeter's thesis, as expounded in his book, *Capitalism, Socialism and Democracy*, see W. Paul Strassmann, "Creative Destruction and Partial Obsolescence in American Economic Development," *Journal of Economic History*, September 1959, pp. 335–349.

CHAPTER IV

The Nineteenth Century: America as Initiator

Although, as we have seen, America relied heavily upon British technology, she also developed an industrial technology possessing certain special features which distinguished it from the technology which had been developed earlier in Great Britain. These features were so special that, by the first half of the 1850s, they were beginning to be admired and borrowed without reservation by Great Britain, already known as "the workshop of the world." Indeed, the British themselves coined the phrase "The American System of Manufacturing" to describe the new technology.

In concentrating our attention, as we will, upon the manufacturing sector, it should be understood that we are examining a sector which was relatively small in the early nineteenth century but which grew at a striking rate during the course of the century and was easily the largest single sector by its end. This growth is apparent in Table 3.

Moreover, within the manufacturing sector, more and more of its resources were devoted to supplying critical machinery inputs which were responsible for the growth in productivity in other sectors of the economy. Successful economic development in the nineteenth century was accompanied by a compositional shift in the stock of capital in favor of machinery.[1]

Table 3

Sector Shares in Commodity Output, 1839–1899 (Percent)

Year	Agriculture	Mining	Manufacturing	Construction
1839	72	1	17	10
1849	60	1	30	10
1859	56	1	32	11
1869	53	2	33	12
1879	49	3	37	11
1889	37	4	48	11
1899	33	5	53	9

Source: Robert Gallman, "Commodity Output, 1839–1899," in William Parker (ed.), *Trends in the American Economy in the Nineteenth Century* (Princeton, N.J.: Princeton University Press, 1960), p. 26.

The point is that technological change in the nineteenth century was both generated and, eventually, institutionalized, in a very special way. It emerged in large measure as an accumulation of solutions to a wide range of technical problems on the part of a group of specialized firms in the manufacturing sector which were uniquely oriented toward these problems. These firms were the producers of capital goods—producers of the machinery and equipment which were used as inputs in the other sectors of the economy. Their growing skill in solving problems in specialized machine production ought to be regarded as the basic learning process underlying nineteenth-

1. Gallman's figures show a sharp rise in manufactured producers' durables as a proportion of the total output of capital goods (i.e., manufactured producers' durables + farm improvements + total construction). This ratio rose from 10 percent in 1839 to 15 percent in 1859, 20 percent in 1879, and stood at 31 percent in 1899. See Gallman, *op. cit.*, p. 36.

century industrialization. Thus, we are by no means in our approach neglecting other sectors, such as transportation, for we are looking at the sector of the economy which produced rolling stock and locomotives for the railroads; nor are we neglecting mining, for the tools and machinery of growing sophistication in mining orginated here; nor are we neglecting agriculture for, in the nineteenth century, productivity growth in agriculture was largely a process of mechanization. (Indeed, the nineteenth-century mechanization of agriculture took place with little shift to new power sources, although there was a considerable substitution of animal power for manpower. Many of the new machines—reaper, steel plow, cultivator, etc. —relied entirely upon traditional animal power.)[2]

2. Mechanization did mean, however, a large-scale substitution of horses for oxen, since the latter did not move swiftly enough to serve as efficient sources of motive power for the new machinery. Thus, whereas in the State of Illinois in 1850 there were about 3.5 horses for each ox, by 1870 this ratio had risen to about 43 horses for each ox. Charles H. Fitch, "Report on the Manufactures of Interchangeable Mechanism," in U.S. Census Office, *Tenth Census: Manufactures*, vol. II, (Washington, D.C. 1883), p. 78.

The major role played by animal power as a source of power supply until the time it was displaced for road transport and agricultural work by the internal combustion engine is too often forgotten. In fact, the number of horses on American farms rose to its peak in the second decade of the twentieth century, after which it declined rapidly, as the following figures show.

Number of Horses on American Farms (Thousands)

1870	7,145
1880	10,357
1890	15,266
1900	16,965
1910	19,220
1920	19,767
1930	13,384
1940	10,087
1945	8,499
1950	5,402
1955	4,309
1957	3,574

Source: *Historical Statistics of the United States, op. cit.*, pp. 289–290.

When the rest of the world first became aware of the existence of a special sort of technology in the U.S., an awareness which we may date with the great Crystal Palace Exhibition in London in 1851, what impressed them most was the existence of a technology which could produce complex mechanisms on an interchangeable basis. Indeed, the phrase coined at this period by the British, "The American System of Manufacturing," referred specifically to the characteristic of interchangeability. That is to say, they were impressed by a method of producing mechanisms possessing closely fitting and interacting components in such a way that a given component of any of the mechanisms would fit and perform equally well, *with no adjustments,* in any of the other mechanisms. Appropriately enough, the British public first observed this interchangeability in a display of American firearms at the Crystal Palace Exhibition. They were so impressed with the firearms that they later sent a parliamentary committee to the U.S. to observe American techniques of firearms making. This committee, in turn, promptly paid the ultimate compliment to American skill: it arranged for the purchase of a large quantity of the machinery for making firearms and installed this machinery in a gunmaking arsenal in England.[3]

In its report on its visit to the U.S. federal armory at Springfield, the committee stated:

The role of steam power in American agriculture is treated in Reynold M. Wik, *Steam Power on the American Farm* (Philadelphia: University of Pennsylvania Press, 1953). Steam became important primarily in the post-harvest operations—threshing and ginning.

3. Indeed, in the next fifteen or twenty years similar American gunmaking machinery was shipped to Russia, Prussia, Spain, Turkey, Sweden, Denmark, Egypt, and other countries. Fitch, *op. cit.,* p. 4.

With regard to the interchange of parts between the machine-made muskets of the United States' Government, which has caused so much discussion, the Committee particularly interested themselves; and with the view of testing this as fully as possible, selected with Colonel Ripley's permission ten muskets, each made in a different year, *viz.*, from 1844 to 1853 inclusive, from the principal arsenal at Springfield, which they caused to be taken to pieces in their presence, and the parts placed in a row of boxes, mixed up together. They then requested the workman, whose duty it is to 'assemble' the arms, to put them together, which he did—the Committee handing him the parts, taken at hazard—with the use of a turnscrew only, and as quickly as though they had been English muskets, whose parts had carefully been kept separate.[4]

The characteristic of interchangeability with which the committee was so preoccupied was indeed a significant one, because a product possessing this feature is necessarily very different from a product where it is absent. For interchangeability vastly simplified the repair of the product as well as its ordinary care and maintenance. This is one of the reasons why the system first arose in firearms manufacture. Under battlefield conditions it was easy to repair or even to reconstruct a damaged weapon if the parts were interchangeable. An army in the field equipped with such weapons is no longer confronted with many of the critical supply problems resulting from dependence upon skilled armorers. No longer were rifles with damaged locks placed aside until the services of an armorer could be procured, at which time the rifle could be repaired or a new part specially made and fitted into place. New parts could now be readily substituted in the field for damaged ones, and it was even possible to "cannibalize" two guns—say, one in which the barrel was damaged—and thus quickly acquire a

4. *Report of the Committee on the Machinery of the U.S.A.*, as reprinted in Rosenberg (ed.), *op. cit.*, pp. 121–122.

usable firearm. The significance of this feature is suggested by a report that, at one point in the Napoleonic Wars (1811) the British government had in its possession some 200,000 musket barrels which were useless because of the absence of a sufficient supply of skilled armorers to make or repair the locks.[5]

This point is of general importance with respect to all interchangeable products. In the absence of the high degree of standardization and precision manufacture of component parts, upon which interchangeability is based, the repair and maintenance of complex products such as automobiles, bicycles, television sets, typewriters, etc., would assume truly nightmarish proportions.

But aside from the usefulness of interchangeability to the owner of the final product, this feature was an essential ingredient of a new and dramatically different technique of manufacture which came to dominate the light metal working industries of the U.S. It was in these industries that American technology developed unique features—of which interchangeability was one—which spread to a progressively wider range of products in the course of the nineteenth and twentieth centuries.

In order to appreciate what was truly significant about the manufacturing methods of the new technology, it is necessary to consider the system which it replaced, essentially one relying upon the developed skills of individual handicraftsmen. In the case of gunmaking, the lock, stock, and barrel were each the work of separate groups of craftsmen. The locks, which were particularly intricate mechanisms, were produced by methods which involved the forging of component parts on an anvil, extensive filing so that individual parts would fit together, and

5. Joseph W. Roe, "Interchangeable Manufacture," *Transactions of the Newcomen Society*, 17 (1936–37): 165.

finishing by means of polishing and hardening. In all this the file was really the indispensable instrument because it was the filing which brought about the fine adjustments which assured that the separate parts would interact properly. The gunstock was one of the most serious bottlenecks in firearms production so long as handicraft methods were employed. Its highly irregular shape seemed to defy the development of effective machine techniques, and the hand-shaping of the stock, employing whittling-knife, chisel and file, was an extremely tedious and costly operation. Indeed, one authority stated that, before the introduction of wood-working machinery, a skilled man was capable of producing only between one and two stocks a day.[6]

For present purposes one of the most distinctive features of gunmaking by craftsmen was the inordinate cost which had to be incurred in combining the component parts into a working, finished product. Because the gun is a complex mechanism, the separate parts must be carefully adjusted to one another if it is to function properly. One way of assuring such adjustment is by achieving a high degree of standardization and precision, but when hand methods are employed this is either impossible or prohibitively costly. In fact, a critical feature of handicraft gunmaking is the very high cost involved in fitting together into a properly working mechanism—primarily by the use of the file —the individual components produced by large numbers of separate craftsmen. Considerable skill and patience were required for such tasks as fitting and recessing the gunstock so that it would properly accommodate the lock and barrel, and correctly arranging the pins and screws. Some sense of the cost of fitting under a handicraft technology may be derived from the fact that, as late as the 1850s in Birmingham, the center of the

6. Fitch, *op. cit.*, p. 14.

British gunmaking trade, there were substantially more workers engaged in finishing and fitting the separate gun components than were engaged in their original manufacture.[7]

A major feature of the new American technology may now
be simply stated: it eliminated or at least substantially reduced
the very costly fitting activities which were an inseparable aspect of the older handicraft system. The new machines were
labor-saving in that they simply eliminated the need for the
highly labor-intensive stage of fitting. A crucial difference between the old and new techniques is the difference between
fitting and assembling. The parliamentary committee, quoted
earlier, was so amazed at this feature that it enclosed the word
"assemble" in quotation marks whenever the word was used
throughout its report.

The workman whose business it is to "assemble" or set up the arms,
takes the different parts promiscuously from a row of boxes, and uses
nothing but the turnscrew to put the musket together, excepting on
the slott, which contains the bandsprings, which have to be squared
out at one end with a small chisel. He receives four cents per musket,
and has put together as many as 100 in a day and 530 in a week, but
his usual day's work is from 50 to 60.
    The time is 3½ minutes.[8]

The fundamental revolution in productive techniques im-
plied by a system under which fitting was abolished and a workman could assemble a musket using "nothing but the turn-

    7. John D. Goodman, "The Birmingham Small Gun Trade," in Samuel Tim-
mins (ed.), *Birmingham and the Midland Hardware District* (London, 1866),
pp. 392–393. According to this source, in the Birmingham gun trade around
1855 there were 3,420 "materials makers" and 3,920 "setters up."
    8. Rosenberg, *op. cit.*, pp. 142–143.

screw" has been insufficiently appreciated. Part of the reason is that we are now so far removed in time from a society where craft skills predominated that we lack an awareness of some of its main cost-generating features. For this reason it is helpful to see the contrast between the old and the new systems through the eyes of the British parliamentary committee. Their report shows clearly their awareness that "assembling" a firearm was a technical innovation of major proportions. Henry Ford, who was later on to bring the system to a more advanced stage of sophistication, also understood the point well. In his article, "Mass Production," which appeared in the twenty-second edition of the *Encyclopaedia Britannica,* he laconically observed: "In mass production there are no fitters."

Interchangeable components, the elimination of dependence upon handicraft skills, and the abolition of extensive fitting operations were, in turn, all aspects of a system whose central characteristic was the design and utilization of highly specialized machinery. It was the ability to invent, design, modify, and produce specialized machinery which linked together these characteristics into a larger system of low-cost mass manufacture of standardized products. Interchangeability, it should be understood, is critical not only because it permits assembly without fitting, but because it makes possible a much higher degree of specialization than would otherwise be possible. Beginning in the production of firearms in the first couple of decades of the nineteenth century, the new system grew in several important ways throughout the rest of the century. First, as the extent of precision in tool operation improved and as cheaper and more effective measurement devices became available, the degree of interchangeability actually achieved on the machine itself increased markedly, and the amount of hand labor, accordingly, declined.[9] Second, the technique of production continued to expand and to absorb an ever-widening range of metal-using products—clocks and watches, sewing machines, agricultural implements, locomotives, locks, hardware, ammunition, typewriters, bicycles and, early in the twentieth century, automobiles. Some of the products of this new technology were household words for generations: Colt revolvers, Jerome clocks, Waltham watches, Yale locks, McCormick reapers, Singer sewing machines, Remington rifles and typewriters.[10] Thirdly, perhaps most important, the production of the specialized machinery itself became a specialized activity undertaken by a well-defined group of firms in the capital goods sector. This last development, the emergence of a new industry capable of designing and producing highly specialized machinery to accommodate the very specific needs of machinery users, is so fundamental to the development of the new technology of "machinofacture" (as Marx appropriately called it) that it demands more detailed examination.[11]

9. Eli Whitney, in working on his government musket contracts in the early years of the nineteenth century, apparently achieved some degree of uniformity among the parts of the gun lock by hand methods, i.e., filing jigs or fixtures were used to provide guidance for files in the hands of workmen. Such procedures are, of course, very costly. See Robert Woodbury, "The Legend of Eli Whitney and Interchangeable Parts," *Technology and Culture,* Summer 1960, pp. 235–253.

10. While all these products were manufactured with the new machine technology and partook of the economies made possible by such machine production, the characteristic of interchangeability was not equally important in all of them. Where moving parts interact, precision and interchangeability are vital. But such characteristics are clearly not relevant, e.g., on the portions of agricultural implements which interact with the soil or with the crops—as in the cases of plows, cultivators, and reapers. The high degree of similarity of measurements among components is, here, an inevitable by-product of the use of specialized machinery.

11. Here again the British parliamentary committee, quoted earlier, perceived this trend in the first half of the 1850s: "As regards the class of machinery

The reason for calling this fundamental is that industrialization, quite simply, requires the development of highly specialized kinds of skills and knowledge which are essential to the solution of the technical problems involved in machine production. In all of this there is an essential learning process and, historically, much of this learning took place within the confines of a small number of firms engaged in machine production. Furthermore, the rapidity of industrialization was substantially determined by the speed with which technical knowledge was diffused from its point of origin to other sectors of the economy where such knowledge had practical applications.[12]

usually employed by engineers and machine makers, they are upon the whole behind those of England, but in the adaptation of special apparatus to a single operation in almost all branches of industry, the Americans display an amount of ingenuity, combined with undaunted energy, which as a nation we would do well to imitate, if we mean to hold our present position in the great market of the world." *Report of the Committee on the Machinery of the U.S.*, as reprinted in Rosenberg, *op. cit.*, pp. 128–129. In reporting upon the Philadelphia Centennial Exhibition in 1876, Mr. John Anderson stated: "To realize the nature of the competition that awaits us, their [American] factories and workshops have to be inspected, in order to see the variety of special tools that are being introduced, both to insure precision and to economize labour; this system of special tools is extending into almost every branch of industry where articles have to be repeated. This applies to furniture, hardware, clocks, watches, small arms, ammunition, and to an endless variety of other things. The articles so made are not only good in quality, but the cost of production is extremely low, notwithstanding that those employed earn high pay." *Reports on the Philadelphia International Exhibition of 1876, Presented to both Houses of Parliament* (1877), 1: 235.

12. Fishlow has emphasized the parallel role of railroad repair shops as a powerful force in the diffusion of mechanical skills in the antebellum years. "It is not my intention to slight ante-bellum locomotive production; the volume of output in the 1850's compares favorably to that in the 1880's and it may be that as a proportion of the entire machinery industry, locomotives did reach their maximum before 1860. Where the railroad had greatest effect, however, was not so much in the rise of specialized locomotive firms from general machine shops as in the development of elaborate repair facilities on the railroads themselves. Here *was* a powerful force for the geographic dissemination of skills necessary to an industrial society. . . . Such shops were numerous because railroads themselves were numerous, and the quality of their furnishings was

The machine tool industry, then, played a unique role *both* in the initial solution of technical problems and in the rapid transmission and application of newly-learned techniques to other uses. In this sense the machine tool industry was a center for the acquisition and diffusion of the skills and techniques uniquely required in a machinofacture type of economy. Its role was a dual one: (1) new skills and techniques were developed here in response to the demands of specific customers, and (2) once acquired, the machine tool industry served as the main transmission center for the transfer of new skills and techniques to the entire machine-using sector of the economy. A wide range of metal-working industries were continually being confronted with similar kinds of problems which urgently required solution and which, once solved by the machinery-producing sector, took their place in short order in the production of other metal-using products employing similar processes.

Around the year 1820 it would have been impossible to identify a distinct collection of firms whose primary activity was the production of machinery. Machines of varying degrees of complexity were, of course, employed in industry, but the production of such machines had not become the specialized function of individual firms. In general, machines were either produced by firms which were engaged in the production of metal or wooden products, and therefore possessed skills and facilities which could be applied to the manufacture of machinery; or

generally of very high standard. . . . [T]he fact is that many railway shops were machine shops in miniature, with their demands for lathes and other machine tools on the one hand, and their training of the labor force on the other. If 5 percent of the operating employees on railroads in 1860 were skilled machinists, and the 1880 census indicated a ratio that large at a later date, the total number employed by the railroads would exceed those employed in locomotive works by more than a fifth!" Fishlow, *American Railroads, op. cit.*, pp. 154–155.

machines were produced by their ultimate users on an *ad hoc* basis. Thus, machinery-producing firms can first be observed, *in embryo,* as adjuncts to textile factories. Such machine-producing shops emerged in the textile firms of New England where they were attached to such firms as the Amoskeag Manufacturing Company in Manchester, New Hampshire, and the Lowell Mills in Lowell, Massachusetts. The more successful of these shops undertook, not only the manufacture of textile machinery for sale to other firms, but the production of a range of other kinds of machinery as well. This included steam engines, turbines, mill machinery, and machine tools. At this early stage, then, skills which had been acquired in the production of one kind of machine were transfered to other sectors by the simple expedient of an expansion and diversification of output on the part of a successful producer of one type of machinery. For example, when the railroads were introduced during the 1830s, the Lowell Machine Shop, which had previously produced textile machinery, undertook to produce locomotives. In this new activity it was highly successful and by the mid-1840s it became independent of its textile origins. Similarly, early locomotives were produced in New Hampshire by the Amoskeag Manufacturing Company; in New Jersey by some of the cotton textile firms in Paterson; and in Philadelphia by the Baldwin Locomotive Works, the most successful of all American locomotive builders, that grew out of a firm whose highly diverse output had earlier included textile-printing machinery. This increasing specialization in machine production, in response to a growing market for machinery, was duplicated elsewhere. Whereas the production of the heavier, general purpose machine tools—lathes, planers, boring machines—was initially undertaken by the early textile machine shops in response to their own internal requirements and those of the new railroad industry, the lighter, more specialized high speed machine tools—turret lathes, milling machines, precision grinders—grew out of the production requirements of the makers of firearms. Somewhat later (roughly 1850–80) a similar role was played by the makers of sewing machines; in the last years of the nineteenth century by the demands of the new bicycle industry and in the first couple of decades of the twentieth century by the demands of the automobile industry.

The machine tool industry originated, then, out of a series of responses to the machinery requirements of a succession of particular industries. While still attached to their industries of origin, these establishments undertook to produce machinery for other industries, because the technical skills which were acquired in the industry of origin had direct applications to production problems in other industries. That this should have been so is hardly surprising, for it is of the essence of industrialization that it involves the introduction of a relatively small number of broadly similar productive processes to a large number of industries. This in turn follows from the fact that industrialization in the nineteenth century involved the growing adoption of a metal-shaping technology which relied increasingly upon decentralized sources of power.[13] Eventually, with

13. The use of machinery in the cutting of metal into precise shapes involves, to begin with, a relatively small number of operations (and therefore machine types): turning, boring, drilling, milling, planing, grinding, polishing, etc. Moreover, all machines performing such operations confront a similar collection of technical problems, dealing with such matters as power transmission (gearing, belting, shafting), control devices, feed mechanisms, friction reduction, and a broad array of problems connected with the properties of metals (such as ability to withstand stresses and heat resistance). It is because these processes and problems became common to the production of a wide range of disparate commodities that industries which were apparently unrelated from the point of view of the nature and uses of the final product became very closely related on a technological basis—for example, firearms, sewing machines, and bicycles.

the combined growth in demand for an increasing array of specialized machines, machine tool production emerged as a separate industry consisting of a large number of firms, most of which confined their operations to a narrow range of products —frequently to a single type of machine tool and with only minor modifications with respect to size, auxiliary attachments, or components.

These developments were recognized in the 1900 census:

In late years . . . manufacturers starting in this branch of industry [metal-working machinery] have very generally limited their operations to the production of a single type of machine, or at the most to one class embracing tools of similar types. For example, there are large establishments in which nothing is manufactured but engine lathes, other works are devoted exclusively to planers, while in others milling machines are the specialty.

This tendency has prevailed in Cincinnati perhaps more than in any other city, and has been one of the characteristic features of the rapid expansion of the machine-tool industry in that city during the past ten years. During the census year there were in Cincinnati 30 establishments devoted to the manufacture of metal-working machinery, almost exclusively of the classes generally designated as machine tools, and their aggregate product amounted to $3,375,436. In 7 shops engine lathes only were made, 2 were devoted exclusively to planers, 2 made milling machines only, drilling machines formed the sole product of 5 establishments, and only shapers were made in 3 shops.[14]

In 1914 the Census of Manufactures reported that there were 409 machine tool establishments in the United States producing an output of $31,446,660.[15] In the same year the *American Machinist*, in a survey which was admittedly incomplete, pub-

14. *Twelfth Census of the United States* (1900), X, Part 4, "Manufactures," p. 385.
15. *Census of Manufactures* (1914), II, "Reports for Selected Industries," p. 269. For the same year there were 277 metal-working machinery plants, other than those producing machine tools, with an output valued at $17,419,526.

lished a map showing the locations of 570 firms engaged in the production of "machine tools, small tools, machinist's tools and machine tool appurtenances. . . ." These firms were all in the northeast quadrant of the country, with Ohio leading with 117, followed by Massachusetts with 98, Connecticut with 66, Pennsylvania with 60, New York with 57, and Illinois with 42.[16]

The importance of the machine tool industry to the process of technical change is that it came to constitute a pool or reservoir of the skills and technical knowledge which were essential to the generation of technical change throughout the machine-using sectors of the economy. Precisely because it came to deal with processes and problems which were common to an increasing number of industries, it played the role of a transmission center in the diffusion of the new technology. The pool of skill and technical knowledge was added to as a result of problems which arose in particular industries. Once the particular problem was solved and added to the pool, the solution became available, with perhaps minor modifications and redesigning, for employment in the growing number of technologically related industries. Alternatively stated, the existence of a well-developed machine tool industry induced a higher rate of technological change by lowering the cost of innovation throughout the metal-using sectors of the economy.

In this fashion a growing family of metal-shaping tools was built up during the nineteenth century. The machines were designed and adapted to perform highly specialized functions. Even though a basic tool was capable of performing a wide range of tasks, it was designed and adapted for the high-speed and increasingly automatic performance of narrowly-defined operations. Moreover, a further aspect of this technology was,

16. *American Machinist*, January 29, 1914, p. 210.

necessarily, a proliferation in the number of specialized machines, since each machine was deliberately designed for high-speed performance of a limited task. This meant a sequential productive process involving large numbers of special-purpose machines, each one of which advanced the product one small step further toward its final shape. Where the demand for the final product was sufficiently large, and where the standardization of the product was sufficient to permit use of inflexible, special-purpose machinery, very low per unit costs were attainable. These two preconditions help to explain why this technology should have originated in the first half of the nineteenth century in the production of military firearms and was quickly applied to clocks and then watches.

Thus we find that Blanchard's stocking lathe, which had been introduced in 1818 to replace the expensive hand processes of whittling, boring, and chiseling in shaping the gunstock, was very soon no longer a single machine, but a *sequence* of machines, each of which performed a small, highly specialized operation.

By 1827 Blanchard's stocking and turning machinery had been developed into 16 machines, in use at both national armouries, and for the following purposes: sawing off stock, facing stock and sawing lengthwise, turning stock, boring for barrel, turning barrel, milling bed for barrel-breech and pin, cutting bed for tang of breech-plate, boring holes for breech-plate screws, gauging for barrel, cutting for plate, forming bed for interior of lock, boring side and tang-pin holes, and turning fluted oval on breech.[17]

The Blanchard technique for reproducing irregular patterns in wood was rapidly transferred to a range of items including hat

17. Fitch, *op. cit.*, p. 14.

blocks, ax handles, ox-yokes, spokes of wheels, oars, shoe lasts, and even sculptured busts.

Because of the vital importance of precision to the success of the new manufacturing methods, much attention was devoted, from the beginning, to techniques which would achieve such precision and thereby guarantee interchangeability. Thus the firearms industry was instrumental in the development of the whole array of tools and accessories upon which the production of precision metal parts was dependent: jigs (originally employed for drilling and hand-filing), fixtures, taps and gauges, and the systematic development of die-forging methods.

The firearms industry was also the source of the milling machine although its exact origins are shrouded in obscurity. This machine was devised as a substitute for hand filing and chiseling operations in shaping the parts of the gun lock. Its multiple rotary cutters provided an extremely rapid and efficient substitute for hand skills in imparting shapes to metal. The design of the plain milling machine was stabilized in the form which came to be known as the Lincoln miller in the 1850s, and rapidly assumed a prominent place in all the metal trades. One authority has estimated that, between 1855 and 1880, " . . . nearly 100,000 of these machines or practical copies of them, have been built for gun, sewing-machine and similar work."[18] The versatility of this machine was greatly increased during the Civil War when the Brown and Sharpe Company of Providence, Rhode Island, a firm which had been engaged in sewing machine production, attempted to develop a new method for making twist drills which were, in turn, required for

---

18. Fitch, *op. cit.*, p. 26. It is interesting to note that the Lincoln miller, which played such an important role in producing components of interchangeable products, was itself composed of interchangeable parts.

producing Springfield muskets. The result was the universal milling machine, which eliminated the need for the hand filing of the twist drills. At the same time this amazingly useful machine could be used in all kinds of spiral milling operations and in gear cutting, as well as in the cutting of all sorts of irregular shapes in metal. Some idea both of its versatility and the speed with which this technique was diffused from its point of origin may be derived from the following information: within ten years after Brown and Sharpe produced the first universal milling machine in 1862, the firm had sold similar machines to manufacturers of hardware, tools, cutlery, locks, arms, sewing machines, textile machinery, printing machines, professional and scientific instruments, locomotives, to machine shops and foundries, and to machine tool manufacturers.[19] In subsequent decades, with each new product innovation, universal milling machines were sold to a succession of firms producing cash registers, calculating machines, typewriters, agricultural implements, bicycles, and automobiles. Furthermore, toward the end of the nineteenth century, heavy-duty milling machines increasingly undertook machining operations previously performed by planing and shaping machines.

The turret lathe, together with the milling machine—the other most important machine in the new metal-shaping technology—had origins somewhat similar to that of the milling machine: it emerged from the firearms industry of New England in the 1840s (some twenty years or so later than the milling machine). It began to be sold commercially in the mid-1850s and underwent innumerable modifications as it was adapted to the production of components for such products as

---

19. In 1880 milling machines constituted between 25 and 30 percent of the total number of machines in use in arms-making factories. Fitch, *op. cit.*, p. 22.

firearms, sewing machines, watches, typewriters, locomotives, hardware, bicycles, and automobiles. The turret lathe, which held a cluster of tools placed on a vertical axis, made it possible to perform a sequence of metal-cutting operations on the workpiece with each separate tool without having to reset or remove the piece from the lathe. Furthermore, since each tool was pre-set, the amount of skill required by the lathe operator was much reduced as compared to the skill required of a machinist working with an ordinary lathe. The turret lathe revolutionized all manufacturing processes which required large numbers of small precision components, such as screws, which were soon being produced on turret lathe machines. The major step toward making the turret lathe automatic was taken by Christopher Spencer, a former Colt employee and inventor of the Spencer rifle. It is difficult to exaggerate the importance of this invention, since the self-adjusting feature of the cam cylinder with adjustable strips, through which automaticity was achieved, was eventually to provide the basis for all modern automatic lathe operations. This technique made it possible to set up a machine so that it would run automatically through the whole cycle of tool engagements for which the turret lathe had been "programmed."

Although, as we have seen, many of the specialized tools had their origin in the production of firearms in the first half of the nineteenth century, by the second half of the century these methods had spread to a large number of metal-using industries. The strategic role which the requirements of firearms production had once played in inducing new inventions was now played by a number of industries: notably by the sewing machine industry after 1850, by the bicycle industry after 1890, and by the automobile industry after 1900. Each of these industries was responsible for techniques which were widely used throughout the metal-using sector, and each new industry borrowed much of the technology of earlier industries. Thus, sewing machine producers drew heavily upon the methods of firearms makers, as did the bicycle manufacturers from the sewing machine manufacturers and, finally, as did the automobile industry from the bicycle industry. The general trend was toward greater specialization in machine design, increasing automaticity and much higher speeds. Higher speeds were enormously facilitated by the introduction of high-speed steel in machine cutting tools after 1900, and by the slightly earlier development of silicon carbide, a highly superior artificial abrasive. The bicycle industry had borrowed grinding techniques from the sewing machine industry, but the introduction of the artificial abrasives converted the grinding machine from an instrument which had been used only to perform finishing operations on components which had acquired their basic shapes on a lathe, to a machine capable of performing heavy production operations. Indeed, the grinding machine in this form became indispensable to the emerging automobile industry because it provided the only technique, at the time, of precision machining of the strong, light alloy steels which played such a prominent part in automobile components. Finally, new techniques were devised for dealing with problems which became increasingly troublesome at higher machine speeds and stresses: the use of ball-bearings and lubrication techniques in friction reduction, new machine tool techniques to meet the rapid growth in demand for cheap, durable gears, etc.

The growing nineteenth-century sophistication in the use of machine technology culminated, in the early twentieth century, in the assembly line system—a system whose contribution to the growth in productivity derived from organizational as well as technical innovations. Its emergence is indelibly associated with the early work of Henry Ford in the automobile industry. The historical roots of this system, however, beyond those already discussed, lie in rather strange and unexpected places, such as grain mills and slaughterhouses.

Oliver Evans, one of America's authentic mechanical geniuses, had in the late eighteenth century perfected a highly labor-saving, continuous flow production process, employing many of the techniques for moving material—endless belt conveyors, screw conveyors, and bucket conveyors—which were to be used in twentieth-century factories. Evans's "factory" was a grain mill in which grain flowed through each of the several milling processes "without human intervention":

In 1783 the model of the automatic mill was complete and in the two following years, 1784–5, the mill itself was built in Redclay Creek valley. This mill could load from either boats or wagons; a scale determined the weight and a screw conveyor (or "endless Archimedean screw" as Evans calls it) carried the grain inside to the point where it was raised to the top storey by a bucket conveyor (or "elevator for raising vertically"). It handled three hundred bushels an hour. From this elevator, the grain fell on the mildly inclined "descender—a broad endless strap of very thin pliant leather, canvas or flannel, revolving over two pulleys." This belt was set in motion by the weight of the grain and, as Evans adds, "it moves on the principle of an overshot waterwheel." A prominent mechanical engineer remarks a century later: "It is the prototype of belt conveyor of the present day, usually used for horizontal movement." After intervening operations, the grain was carried down to the millstones and from the millstones back to the top storey. Thus it made its way . . . through all the floors, from bottom to top and top to bottom, much as the automobile bodies in Henry Ford's plant of 1914.[20]

20. Giedion, *Mechanization Takes Command, op. cit.*, p. 82. Illustrations of Evans's mill appear on pp. 81 and 83.

Appropriately enough for a country which was still primarily agricultural, the next major step forward in mechanical materials handling also dealt with food processing. In the slaughterhouses of Cincinnati the "disassembly" of pigs was carried out by a technique involving workmen at fixed stations while a system of overhead rails suspended from the ceiling moved the carcass, hanging from a hook, at a carefully predetermined rate, from one phase to the next. Each man performed a single operation: one split the animal, the next removed its entrails, another removed specific organs—heart, liver, etc.—and the last man washed down the carcass with a hose. Although it was impossible to eliminate the reliance upon the human eye and human skill in the slaughter-house,[21] the skillful handling of materials, the rationalized positioning of the workers, the elimination of time loss between operations, the minimization of energy expended by the workers in handling heavy carcasses, and the minute subdivision of labor brought about very substantial increases in the productivity of labor. This system was certainly in existence in Cincinnati packinghouses in 1860 and may even have been there, in somewhat more primitive form, as much as twenty-five years earlier.[22]

21. "[I]n the slaughtering process the material to be handled is a complex, irregularly shaped object: the hog. Even when dead, the hog largely refuses to submit to the machine. Machine tools for planing iron, undeviating to the millionth of an inch, could be constructed around 1850. Down to the present day, no one has succeeded in inventing a mechanism capable of severing the ham from the carcass. We are dealing here with an organic material, ever changing, ever different, impossible to operate upon by revolving cutters. Hence all the essential operations in the mass production of dressed meat have to be performed by hand." Giedion, *op. cit.*, pp. 93–94.

22. See Kouwenhoven, *Made in America, op. cit.*, pp. 38–40. The general neglect, often amounting to disdain, of the food processing industries in the course of industrialization is curious and difficult to understand. As a result of this neglect we are most ill-informed concerning the economic history of this significant sector of the economy. For some recent salutary remarks on the

America's sophisticated techniques of handling materials caught the attention of many observers. One sharp-eyed Scandinavian immigrant was particularly struck by the operation of Chicago's grain elevators, one of which he described in the following terms:

Here is a solid stone building erected on a pile foundation right at the river's edge, with water on three sides; a building 203 feet long, 101 feet wide, and 117 feet high. As one enters one is puzzled by a vast number of beams and iron rods which cross each other in every direction, partly to give strength to the structure, partly to form its seven stories. Along one wall run two railroad tracks, spurs from a great nearby main line which, branching out in every direction, connects Chicago with the most fertile grain regions in Illinois and other sections along the Mississippi River. On each of these spurs, six freight cars can be hauled into the elevator for unloading at one time. For that purpose two elevators have been built near the two tracks, and by means of them a train of wheat or corn can.be emptied in six minutes —though ten minutes is the regular time in which the load is lifted from the cars and dumped into the grain bins. In the building are 148

subject, see Fishlow, *American Railroads, op. cit.,* pp. 225–230. Fishlow states: "The processing industries were more important, to American industrialization at least, than has usually been assumed. The high capital-output ratios are not without technological significance. In 1870, the first census to record horsepower revealed the milling industry as the single largest industrial user of power in the United States. Virtually a fourth of the total industrial horsepower was developed by it. But this is not all. It developed four times the steam power of the cotton industry and exceeded the iron industry in this respect as well. . . ." Fishlow also points out that the growth of the food processing industry in the late nineteenth century was a significant force in the spread of industrial technology. "It immediately disseminated a modern technology to the interior, predominantly agricultural parts of the country. . . . It introduced the beginnings of industrialization in a natural and automatic way. Subsequent transition to a more sophisticated industrial structure became the easier. The westward movement of milling, of meat packing, and of tanning in response to shifts in the sources of supply contributed to the rise of such urban areas as Cincinnati, Chicago, St. Louis, Minneapolis-St. Paul, Omaha, and Kansas City. In a context of progressive agriculture, industrialization may be eased rather than hindered by the lure of high returns in farming."

such bins, each one 50 feet deep and with a capacity of 5,000 bushels of grain. A carload is generally 350 bushels. After the elevator has gathered up the grain from the car it empties it into a big 500-bushel scoop which is hoisted up to one of the upper stories where it is placed on a scale. After the weight of the 500 bushels has been ascertained, the bottom of the scoop is opened and its contents drop into one of the grain bins. The scoop is immediately lowered to be refilled and once more hoisted. All of this, including the weighing, is done with great speed. Through a simple contrivance 12 to 16 bins may be filled with a single scoop. And so, in ten minutes the grain from a train loaded with about 3,000 bushels is raised by 12 elevators, weighed, and transferred to the bins.

If a vessel is to be loaded it is brought to the side of the elevator, a lid in the bottom of the bin is opened, and the grain runs into the elevator to be hoisted up and weighed, 500 bushels at a time being placed on the scale, whereupon it is run through a spout into the hold of the vessel. All this is done with almost incredible speed. At the time the cars are being unloaded at one side of the elevator, the grain may, if necessary, after it has been hoisted up and weighed, be loaded into the vessel on the other side, to be exported. Thus in less than an hour two ships are loaded with 12,000 bushels apiece.[23]

The automobile assembly lines which were introduced in Detroit in the second decade of the twentieth century thus embodied several historical trends and applied them to a highly complicated product, containing thousands of separate parts, many of which move and interact at high speeds. Henry Ford tentatively experimented with a conveyor-belt system for the assembly of magnetos in 1913. Similar methods were quickly applied to chassis assembly. Much experimentation was carried out in determining optimum assembly line speeds, the best positioning of workmen, most convenient height for the performance of each task, most efficient methods of material routing,

23. *A Pioneer in Northwest America 1841–1858: The Memoirs of Gustaf Unonius*, 2 vols. (Minneapolis, Minn.: Lund Press, 1950), 2: 185.

machine layout, etc. By 1916 the Ford Motor Company alone was selling well over half a million Model Ts at a retail price of less than $400.[24] Seven years later the total number of passenger cars produced in the United States was 3.6 million[25] (see Table 4). Such output volumes would have been unattainable without the rationalization of the work process, particularly the technique of progressive assembly of parts, involving the systematic use of mechanical conveyors in the movement of materials.[26] These techniques were applied in turn to a widen-

24. "When the history of automobile design is someday written, the Model-T Ford will surely turn out to have been one of the most effective contributions to the evolution of a distinctively automotive design. Here was a naked, undisguised machine for transportation, as free from extraneous ornament, as perfectly adapted to mass-production techniques of manufacture as its modern successor in popular affection, the honest-to-God army jeep. If there ever was an unabashed product of the vernacular tradition as this book has defined it, the Model-T Ford was it." Kouwenhoven, *op. cit.*, p. 179.

25. The huge expansion in surfaced roads to accommodate the requirements of the automobile is shown in Table 5. It is interesting to note that, in establishing the interchangeability of components in the American car, a British audience was treated to a display exactly like the one offered to the British parliamentary commission studying American techniques of firearm production fifty years earlier. In 1913 ". . . Henry M. Leland took three American-made Cadillac cars to the Brooklands race track, in England, ran them around the track, had them dismantled, withdrew 91 parts from the heap, substituted 91 identical stock parts, and had the cars reassembled with screw drivers and wrenches as the only tools employed. The cars were then immediately driven 500 miles around the course at an average speed of 35 to 40 miles per hour." R. C. Epstein, *The Automobile Industry* (Chicago: A. W. Shaw and Co., 1928), p. 35.

26. Henry Ford summarized the essential features of the new factory organization as follows: "As to shop detail, the keyword to mass production is simplicity. Three plain principles underlie it: (a) the planned orderly and continuous progression of the commodity through the shop; (b) the delivery of work instead of leaving it to the workman's initiative to find it; (c) an analysis of operations into their constituent parts. These are distinct but not separate steps; all are involved in the first one. To plan the progress of material from the initial manufacturing operation until its emergence as a finished product involves shop planning on a large scale and the manufacture and delivery of material, tools and parts at various points along the line. To do this successfully

ing range of products: numerous products connected with the electrical industry—motors, washing machines, refrigerators, telephones, radios—and a further assortment of consumer durables; many producer durables such as farm machinery and equipment; and food processing.

Furthermore, the productive process itself has been made increasingly automatic, a direction of development for which the term "automation" was coined after the Second World War. Individual machines have been made fully automatic, as in the use of numerical control systems, which program and guide the machine tool through its sequence of operations. Whereas highly automatic machinery had previously been devised which repeated single operations and were therefore appropriate for very long runs, numerically controlled machines now make possible the automation of a sequence of processes on a machine, processes which are themselves continually changing.[27] More-

with a progressing piece of work means a careful breaking up of the work into the sequence of its 'operations.' All three fundamentals are involved in the original act of planning a moving line production." Henry Ford, "Mass Production," *Encyclopaedia Britannica,* 22d edition.

27. "Numerical control is probably the most significant new development in manufacturing technology since Henry Ford introduced the concept of the moving assembly line. It brings to job shop production many of the manufacturing economies now available only with highly automated production systems. Although numerical control has applications in many areas of manufacturing, for example, assembling and wiring electronic circuit boards and producing engineering drawings and flame-cutting metal templates, its most significant application is in the control of metal-cutting machine tools. Numerical control provides instructions to these machine tools in the form of coded instructions punched on paper tape. These instructions control the operation of the machine, position the item to be machined, and select the proper cutting tools for each operation. They enable the machine tool itself to perform most of the functions that are done by the machine operator on conventional machine tools." Frank Lynn, "An Investigation of the Rate of Development and Diffusion of Technology in Our Modern Industrial Society," in *National Commission on Technology, Automation and Economic Progress* (Washington, D.C. U.S.G.P.O., 1966), vol. 2, p. 89.

Table 4

Factory Sales of Passenger Cars

Year	Number
1900	4,192
1901	7,000
1902	9,000
1903	11,235
1904	22,130
1905	24,250
1906	33,200
1907	43,000
1908	63,500
1909	123,990
1910	181,000
1911	199,319
1912	356,000
1913	461,500
1914	548,139
1915	895,930
1916	1,525,578
1917	1,745,792
1918	943,436
1919	1,651,625
1920	1,905,560
1921	1,468,067
1922	2,274,185
1923	3,624,717
1924	3,185,881
1925	3,735,171
1926	3,692,317
1927	2,936,533
1928	3,775,417
1929	4,455,178
1930	2,787,456
1935	3,273,874
1940	3,717,385
1945	69,532
1950	6,665,863
1955	7,920,186
1960	6,675,000
1965	9,306,000
1966	8,598,000

Source: *Historical Statistics of the U.S.*, and *Statistical Abstract of U.S.*, 1967.

Table 5

U.S. Miles of Surfaced Road
(1,000 Miles)

Year	Miles
1904	154
1905	161
1910	204
1915	276
1920	369
1925	521
1930	694
1935	1,080
1940	1,367
1945	1,721
1950	1,939
1955	2,273
1957	2,371

Source: *Historical Statistics of U.S., op. cit.,* p. 458.

over, electronic control devices—employing feedback mechanisms—have eliminated the necessity for human supervision of or intervention in a wide range of productive processes.[28] "Detroit-type" automation has exploited automatic work transfer and positioning devices to link together the operation of successive machines.[29]

28. "What the feedback and the vacuum tube have made possible is not the sporadic design of individual automatic mechanisms, but a general policy for the construction of automatic mechanisms of the most varied type." Norbert Wiener, *The Human Use of Human Beings* (Boston: Houghton Mifflin, 1954), p. 153.
29. See George Terborgh, *The Automation Hysteria* (New York: W. W. Norton and Co., 1966), for a sensible and balanced essay on the economic implications of automation. What Terborgh appropriately calls the "hysteria" of the mid-1960s seems now to have subsided.

The analogue to mass production in the preparation and transformation of materials is continuous process manufacturing, involving large capital expenditures upon highly specialized plant and equipment. Here, as in mass production, low per unit costs are achieved only when it is possible to produce a large volume of a standardized product. Such continuous process technologies are now common in the chemicals, petroleum, steel, aluminum, and cement industries.

CHAPTER V

The Twentieth Century

If the widening scope of mechanization and the diffusion of a machine technology provided a unifying theme for our approach to technological change in the nineteenth century, no such similar key or common denominator is available for the twentieth century. Indeed, the sheer diversity in the sources of technological change is one of the most distinctive features of the twentieth century. It does appear possible, however, to discern a trend underlying this diversity, a trend which can be most conveniently thought of as tracing its origins to the 1860s. That is, an increasing proportion of technological changes have been dependent upon prior advances in systematized knowledge, a knowledge which has brought with it a much more deeply-rooted understanding of the forces of nature and the physical universe. This is a *trend* which, moreover, begins in the second half of the nineteenth century and therefore the contrast between the nineteenth and twentieth centuries should not be overstated. There was a considerable reliance upon science in the inventive process in some areas in the nineteenth century, and there has been much inventive activity in the twentieth century which remains totally innocent of any reliance upon science.[1] The trend, however, is sufficiently pervasive and far advanced that it has altered the whole man vs. environment confrontation in a way which now gives the human agent much more initiative in the adaptive process than he formerly possessed. This shift in the composition of inventive activity away from the empirically-based and toward the newer science-based industries is apparent in the patent statistics. For the period 1916–45 it has been shown that the number of patents granted annually grew much more rapidly in classes dependent upon the application of knowledge from scientific disciplines such as chemistry and physics, whereas the growth in classes dependent upon empirical or practical knowledge and mechanical ingenuity has been much slower.[2] As a more general index of the growing reliance upon inputs of systematized knowledge, it may be pointed out that the number of scientists and technologists has been growing more rapidly than the labor force as a whole since 1870.[3]

The machine-based technology which emerged in the nineteenth century owed relatively little to scientific knowledge. As A. P. Usher has pointed out: "At the lower levels, mechanical invention involves little more than some improvement in the

1. See, e.g., John Jewkes, David Sawers, and Richard Stillerman, *The Sources of Invention* (New York: St. Martin's Press, 1958), chap. 3.

2. Alfred B. Stafford, "Is the Rate of Invention Declining?" *American Journal of Sociology*, May 1952, pp. 539–545. This article is a summary of Stafford's University of Chicago doctoral dissertation, "Trends of Invention in Material Culture" (1950, unpublished). On the basis of the data in this dissertation, Schmookler states: " . . . [B]etween 1916 and 1945 the number of patents granted annually in different Patent Office classes of invention changed at rates of from −10.8 to 13.1 per cent per year, with empirical invention at the low and scientific invention at the high end of the spectrum." Schmookler, *op. cit.*, p. 39. For data showing the increasing reliance in inventive activity upon men trained in science and engineering, see *Ibid.*, Appendix B.

3. U.S. National Science Foundation, *Trends in the Employment and Training of Scientists and Engineers*, NSF-56-11, May 1956.

skills required for the making of simple tools, and as long as invention is essentially empirical, even the development of relatively complex mechanisms does not seem to involve abstract thought or organized scientific knowledge."[4] Usher's observation is particularly applicable to those standardized products at which American technology excelled in the nineteenth century: firearms, clocks, sewing machines, hardware, agricultural implements, bicycles, etc. To a great extent, as we have seen, the necessary skills and techniques were developed in, and diffused by, the machine tool industry. Although mechanization as a source of new technology has continued with great force into the twentieth century, a succession of new sources has developed—chemical, electrical, electronic, biological, and nuclear—each of which has been dependent upon the mastery of complex bodies of knowledge and none of which could have been achieved by the crude empiricism and trial-and-error methods of earlier generations. This contrast between old and new was notably apparent in metallurgy, most particularly in the production of iron and steel, the basic material inputs upon which industrial societies have been constructed. Nineteenth-century industrialization in fact witnessed the continuous substitution of massive quantities of iron and, later, steel, for other materials, such as wood and stone. The production of iron and steel was also an area where America had made no advances over British industrial leadership in the first half of the nineteenth century, and where the New World continued to rely upon the transfer of basic innovations originating in the Old. In order to understand what is so novel and significant about the twentieth-century approach to technologi-

---

4. A. P. Usher, *A History of Mechanical Inventions* (Boston: Beacon Press, 1959) p. 56.

cal change, a brief backward glance is necessary.

Technical progress in metallurgy, an activity which is fundamental to man's tool-making and tool-using abilities, has always been based upon essentially trial-and-error procedures. These procedures did permit a slow and stumbling progress. Men had been smelting iron ores since the third millennium B.C. and the Hittites were making extensive use of iron (and even some use of steel) in the second millennium B.C. with no knowledge of oxidation or reduction. Several techniques for hardening metals had been successfully employed in antiquity even though the actors were entirely unaware that the methods were simply, as one authority has put it, "... different ways of producing imperfections in the regularity of the stacking of atoms in the metal crystals."[5] Indeed, it was not until 1774 that the critical role of carbon in determining the varying properties of wrought iron, cast iron, and steel was finally established.[6] But long before this the swordmakers of Damascus and Japan had learned how to fashion their magnificent products through centuries of trial-and-error methods.

Important technological breakthroughs were possible, employing no more than a crude empiricism, so long as inducements existed for large numbers of individuals to experiment with untried techniques and to employ novel material inputs. If a particular technique or input was superior to others, someone would eventually stumble upon it, however wasteful and inefficient the search process was, just as a sufficiently large number of prospectors with even a small amount of geological knowledge was "bound to" turn up the more accessible veins of gold in the Yukon. It was in this manner that one of the

5. C. S. Smith, "Materials and the Development of Civilization and Science," *Science*, 14 May 1965, p. 911.
6. C. S. Smith, "The Discovery of Carbon in Steel," *Technology and Culture*, Spring 1964, pp. 149–175.

epoch-making innovations of the British industrial revolution came about. The "pay-off" to someone who could successfully smelt iron with a mineral fuel instead of charcoal had long been obvious and had been attempted with uniform lack of success by ironmasters—Sturtevants, Rovensons, Dudleys—throughout the seventeenth century. Abraham Darby succeeded, in 1709, in substituting coke for charcoal in his blast furnace at Coalbrookdale in Shropshire. Success in this particular location owed much to the combination of circumstances that coal was easily accessible near the surface but more important, as mentioned earlier, was of a chemical composition which made it appropriate for smelting purposes.[7] Even though the chemical transformations in iron refining were not understood, strong economic incentives were eventually successful in uncovering new techniques as well as the raw materials which were appropriate to these techniques.[8]

The advance of metallurgical technique ahead of scientific understanding culminated with Bessemer's report of his strikingly successful steelmaking experiments to the meeting of the British Association for the Advancement of Science in August

7. Although it is not usually thought of in such terms, concern with problems of raw material supply was at the heart of the Industrial Revolution. It was the increasingly urgent need to provide a cheap substitute for wood fuel, beginning early in the seventeenth century, which eventually led to the cheap supplies of fuel, power, and iron products upon which early industrial societies were built. The development of techniques which permitted the substitution of coal for wood was therefore a critical step. The steam engine, which made generally available a cheap, decentralized source of power, had originated in turn as a device for pumping water out of increasingly deep coal mines. The development of techniques for substituting coal for wood took some two centuries and James Watt's steam engine was the culmination of over one hundred years of active experimentation and improvement. See A.P. Usher, *op. cit.*, chap. XIII; John Nef, "Coal Mining and Utilization," in vol. III of Singer et al., *A History of Technology, op. cit.*; and E.A. Wrigley, "The Supply of Raw Materials in the Industrial Revolution," *Economic History Review*, August 1962, pp. 1–16.

8. Ashton, *Iron and Steel in the Industrial Revolution, op. cit.*; chaps. 1 and 2.

1856. British ironmakers who had quickly purchased lease rights to the Bessemer process found, to their dismay, that they could not employ it successfully. It so happened that Bessemer had conducted all his experiments with the use of Swedish charcoal iron, the purest form of pig iron which was available to him. Bessemer's technique, however, worked only when certain chemical conditions were precisely fulfilled, and it was a complete failure with ores containing even very slight traces of phosphorus. This as we saw earlier, was not immediately understood, and it was in fact the determination to establish the causes of failure which led to a prolonged, systematic study of the chemical processes involved in iron and steel production. The next major innovation in steelmaking, the "basic" process developed by the chemists Thomas and Gilchrist in 1878, was a direct outcome of these studies. Through their examination of the chemical processes involved in steel production, Gilchrist and Thomas were able to develop a technique for refining iron which, among other things, made it possible to utilize major sources of iron ore whose phosphorus content had precluded their use in the Bessemer process.

In a very real sense, modern metallurgical science may be said to have begun in this immediate post-Bessemer period. It rested upon an inquiry into the basic structure and composition of metals which had been initiated by difficulties which were experienced in the production of iron and steel. The ability to conduct this inquiry was immensely advanced by technological innovation in other spheres. Most important was Henry Clifton Sorby's development, in 1863, of a technique for examining metals under a microscope, by the use of reflected light. It was a technique which immediately opened the door to an understanding of the microstructure of steel. "From steel, the technique spread to show the behavior of microcrystals of the nonferrous metals during casting, working, and annealing. By 1900 it had been proved that most of the age-old facts of metal behavior (which had first been simply attributed to the nature of the metals and had later been partially explained in terms of composition) could best be related to the shape, size, relative distribution, and interrelationships of distinguishable microconstituents."[9]

Another fundamental improvement in experimental technique which was first announced in 1912 was the discovery and application of X ray diffraction and its application to the study of solids. For ". . . it at once gave a measurable physical meaning to structure on an atomic scale, and made this as real as the larger-scale structures that had been revealed by Sorby's microscopic methods half a century earlier. It was a physicist's method par excellence, and a fundamental one, which served to relate much of the unconnected data of the chemist and the metallurgist."[10]

These improvements in experimental techniques, originating in metallurgy, contributed to and joined with the wider stream of understanding of all materials. (Indeed, in recent years this merger is receiving explicit terminological recognition in the substitution of the term "materials science" for "metallurgy.") This broader, fundamental advance in our understanding of the physical world derives from our insight into

9. C. S. Smith, "Materials and the Development of Civilization and Science," *Science*, 14 May 1965, p. 915. The same author has remarked elsewhere that ". . . the structure-property relationship has been the central theme of the last century of metallurgy. . . . While the atom and its substructures are undoubtedly at the bottom of it all, the properties of materials that are experienced and exploited by man are most directly a result of the level of structure represented by the molecule and the microcrystal." Cyril Stanley Smith, (ed.) *The Sorby Centennial Symposium on the History of Metallurgy* (New York: Gordon and Breach, 1965), p. xvii.

10. C.S. Smith, "Materials," *Scientific American*, September 1967, p. 75.

the atomic and molecular basis for the behavior of *all* matter —an understanding which dates from Mendelejeff's formulation of his periodic table of the elements in 1869. Mendelejeff's periodic law and classification not only provided the basis for explaining the properties of the known elements, but it also correctly *predicted* the properties of elements which were unknown at the time, for example, gallium, germanium, and scandium. In more recent years high school textbooks confidently inform their readers of the existence of elements—Alabamine and Virginium—even though these elements have not been isolated. The knowledge revolution in materials science of the past century is based upon a continuous deepening of our understanding of the general rules determining how atoms and molecules combine together into progressively larger and more complex groups.[11] Once these rules are mastered it becomes possible to manipulate materials, to alter their characteristics, to maximize desirable properties, and even to create entirely new and synthetic materials with desired *combinations* of properties. Our recently acquired knowledge of molecular architecture makes it possible to create synthetic materials with combinations of properties which have no counterparts in the natural world.[12] The burgeoning new industries exploiting these man-made organic polymers—the vast range of plastics, synthetic fibers, packaging materials, synthetic rubber, lightweight thermal insulation, water-repellant coating, and high-strength adhesives—are the direct, legitimate offspring of this knowledge of high polymer chemistry.

11. "Foremost in the new understanding of materials is the realization that the properties of all types of materials arise from their structure, from the manner in which their constituent atoms aggregate into hierarchies of molecular or crystalline order or into disordered amorphous structures." *Ibid.*, p. 76.

12. Leo Baekeland created the highly versatile material, Bakelite, out of phenol and formaldehyde in 1907. Bakelite was the first deliberately man-made giant molecule.

It is important to note that the basis for technical progress in these industries is totally unlike that in the old metallurgical industries where trial-and-error and intelligent empiricism led to considerable advances over the centuries. No conceivable amount of experimentation, such as once brought slow progress to metallurgy, could ever have generated modern synthetic polymers.[13] The production of polymers, for example, absolutely required an adequate theory of molecular structures,[14] and a full appreciation of the staggering complexity of these structures in turn required a highly sophisticated collection of instruments—X ray diffraction equipment, the ultra-centrifuge, electron microscope, viscometer, etc. Similarly, the remarkable advances in the electronics industry after the Second World War—the breakthrough in semiconductor technology at Bell Laboratories in 1947–48—with the development of the transistor, the replacement of the vacuum tube by the transistor, the application of semiconductor devices to electronic data processing and to an expanding field of military and commercial uses—were dependent not only upon complex techniques of instrumentation but also upon the development of quantum mechanics in the mid-1920s. For quantum mechanics provided the essential theory which made it possible to understand the

13. Nor could any amount of experimentation with silkworms and mulberry leaves ever have led to the development of nylon and other synthetic fibres.
14. Much of the basic scientific work on the relationship between the structure and the properties of synthetic materials was done by Wallace H. Carothers while he worked for Du Pont from 1928 until his death in 1937. See, for example, chap. IX, "Polymerization," in *The Collected Papers of Wallace H. Carothers on High Polymeric Substances* (New York: Interscience Publishers, 1940), where he discusses solubility properties, mechanical properties, and crystallinity as they relate to structure. This paper, written in 1931, together with Staudinger's finding in 1935 that polymerization involves three distinct steps: (1) chain initiation, (2) chain growth, and (3) chain termination, provided the basic theoretical understanding which made it possible to produce plastics with pre-determined characteristics.

determinants of electrical conductivity in terms of the atomic structure of crystalline solids.[15]

Furthermore, the growing usefulness of knowledge of chemical processes to the transformation of materials has greatly expanded the industrial area over which such knowledge is now relevant. All industrial activity which changes the nature of its material inputs is, in effect, dealing with a chemical process. In this sense,

> ... chemical industries include practically all metallurgical refining; all refinement of fuels such as petroleum, natural gases, and coal; the processes of refining materials leading to the production of cement, rubber (whether "natural" rubber or other basic raw-materials) glass, etc.; and all industries, in short, engaged either in breaking down the molecular or atomic structure of materials into their physical components (analysis), or in reassembling them to make new compounds or materials (synthesis). The emphasis is on the *nature of the process,* and not upon the type or state of raw or unfinished materials. It makes no difference whether the activating agents be heat, electricity, catalysts,

15. A recent publication of the National Academy of Sciences emphasized the dependence of much of our advanced technology upon developments in solid-state physics in the following terms: "Solid-state physics is indispensable in numerous technological developments, such as computers, nuclear reactors, electronics, communications materials and lasers. Typical examples in electronics are the well-known semiconductor devices such as diodes and transistors, and magnetic memory. In fact, the whole communications technology is being fundamentally affected by these developments: electronic telephone switching systems have become practical because of solid-state electronic devices; transmission systems, both analog and pulse-code modulation are being strongly influenced by solid-state devices; transoceanic satellite communication is totally dependent on solid-state electronics devices, which serve not only as active transmission devices and as control devices in rocket boosters but also in the form of solar cells that provide the prime electrical power required for satellite operation. Our present space effort would be impossible without the power, reliability and volume-weight advantages of solid-state electronics. Other areas of technology in which solid-state physics plays a vital role are power-generation and power-conversion techniques that are currently being investigated in the laboratory." National Academy of Sciences—National Research Council, *Physics: Survey and Outlook* (Washington, D.C.: G.P.O., 1966), p. 69.

or bacteria; so long as a change is effected in molecular or atomic structure—so long as the material undergoes inner transformation— the process is a chemical process.[16]

The effect of the knowledge revolution upon agriculture has been, in many ways, strikingly similar to its effect upon materials. Since biological processes are intimately involved, technological adaptation and improvements in agriculture have always reflected a quite explicit Darwinian mechanism of random variation and natural selection. Human intervention in this area until quite recently had very little to do with new knowledge of the biological processes involved. It took the form primarily of a rather blind experimentation with seed varieties in new ecological environments, small variations in technique of planting and cultivation, and breeding methods that were haphazard or guided by mistaken principles. The success of a particular crop often depends upon a delicate combination of environmental qualities—topography, rainfall, chemical composition of the soil, temperature variations, amount of sunlight, etc. Many cereal strains, for example, are so highly photosensitive that they will fail when transferred relatively short distances from one latitude to another. But so long as large numbers of individual agriculturalists were continuously engaged in productive activities involving minor variations in practice, and so long as a reasonably effective communications network existed among them, market forces could be relied upon to select and to diffuse the best practices.[17] This process of modification and adaptation has been particularly evident in the settlement of virgin regions where populations are pushing

16. Robert A. Brady, *Organization, Automation and Society* (Berkeley, Calif.: University of California Press, 1961), p. 203. Emphasis Brady's.

17. See William Parker, "Sources of Agricultural Productivity in the Nineteenth Century," *Journal of Farm Economics,* December 1967, pp. 1455–1468.

out into areas involving new combinations of soil, terrain, and climate, such as the westward movement of the American settlers. This adaptation is well exemplified by the settlement of the American prairies, an environment quite alien to the cultural heritage of Western European settlers.[18] Many serious blunders were committed, partly because of the unfamiliarity to the settlers of such environmental peculiarities as substantial variations in annual rainfall. Out of a prolonged period of experimentation, however, certain plants and animals were found to possess biological capabilities well-suited for survival in different parts of this environment. The British Hereford proved to be the best-suited of the various breeds of beef cattle over the widest area of the plains, whereas Indian Brahman cattle were found to be better adapted to the special climate of the hot, dry Southern plains. Experimentation with the available range of wheat varieties eventually established the clear adaptive superiority of the hard spring and winter wheats of Eastern Europe.[19] Similarly, the experimental process led to the selection and introduction of African and Asiatic sorghums and Mediterranean alfalfa.[20] It is essential to note about these trans-

18. For a masterly social history of the movement of settlers from the eastern woodlands into the unfamiliar, treeless, semi-arid environment beyond the 98th meridian, see Walter Prescott Webb's *The Great Plains* (Boston: Ginn and Co., 1931). Webb carefully documents the process of experimentation and invention through which new weapons were adopted; new techniques developed for making fences, providing water and farming; and new institutions devised and old ones modified as settlers made the gradual transition from woodcraft to plainscraft in the vast expanse of the Great American Desert.

19. The hard red winter wheat was brought to the United States by a small group of Mennonites who had emigrated to Kansas from southern Russia in 1873.

20. See the works of James C. Malin, especially *Winter Wheat* (Lawrence, Kansas: University of Kansas Press, 1944); *The Grassland of North America* (Lawrence, Kansas, 1947); and *Grassland Historical Studies* (Lawrence, Kansas, 1950). A useful brief statement of Malin's views are given in his article, "Ecology and History," *Scientific Monthly*, May 1950, pp. 295–298.

fers, however, that no alterations were consciously made in the biological characteristics of the plants and animals involved. Indeed, the biological mechanisms were not understood, and existing knowledge in the late nineteenth century certainly did not provide a sufficient basis for a more active human intervention in the adaptive process such as is involved in hybridization and genetic mutation.[21] Modern genetics, which has provided the theoretical basis for the plant and animal breeding underlying much of the recent growth in agricultural productivity, may be said to have begun with the work of Mendel in the mid-1860s, who established mathematical laws of inheritance in accounting for the characteristics of garden peas. Mendel's work was ignored for the remainder of the nineteenth century, but became the starting point for the study of heredity in the twentieth century. In spite of the absence of an adequate knowledge base, trial-and-error experimentation in the nineteenth century was successful in introducing crops and livestock whose existing characteristics made them well suited for survival in the peculiar conditions of the sub-humid grasslands of America.[22]

21. Of course some selective breeding of animals had long been practiced and it, too, yielded results even though it was based upon a crude empiricism. The mule, after all, is a very old hybrid.

22. For a highly illuminating account of the transfer of western hemisphere crops to the "old world" in the sixteenth and seventeenth centuries—a transfer which had enormous social and economic consequences—see G. B. Masefield, "Crops and Livestock," in E. E. Rich and C.H. Wilson (eds.), *The Cambridge Economic History of Europe*, Vol. 4, *The Economy of Expanding Europe in the 16th and 17th Centuries* (Cambridge: Cambridge University Press, 1967), pp. 275–301. The great significance of these transfers is indicated by Masefield as follows: "It was the unforeseen discovery of America which changed the agricultural map of the world. As Columbus and his successors became familiar with the agriculture of America, they found that the only crops common to both the Old and New Worlds were cotton, coconuts and some gourds. The crops hitherto unknown outside America included maize, cassava, potatoes, sweet potatoes (which may or may not have reached some of the Pacific islands by this date), groundnuts, French beans, tobacco, cocoa, pineapples and tomatoes. The

A large part of the social, political, and economic history of the United States could be written around the bare statistical information that the proportion of the American labor force in agriculture was 63 percent in 1840 and 8 percent in 1960.[23] But whereas in the nineteenth century the main sources of productivity growth which made this transformation possible were primarily mechanization, transportation improvements, and regional crop specialization, in the last few decades it is increasingly based upon the growth of knowledge dealing with the fundamental biological processes of life and growth—especially genetics and biochemistry. This recently-accumulated intellectual capital enables the human agent to assert an initiative in growth processes which was never before possible. Instead of experimenting with *existing* seed strains to determine which one is best adapted to the ecological conditions of a given locality, it is now possible, once local requirements have been ascertained, to *create* new seed strains possessing the desired characteristics.

The commercial introduction of hybrid corn in the United States beginning in the early 1930s provided dramatic evidence of the potential benefits from this new biological sophistica-

dog was the only domestic animal common to both hemispheres; otherwise the Americans had only partially domesticated the llama, the guinea-pig, and the turkey.

"Thus at one stroke the potential vegetable resources of the known world had been doubled. The dispersal of crops and livestock which followed was the most important in human history, and perhaps had the most far-reaching effects of any result of the discoveries. Without the American crops, Europe might not have been able to carry such heavy populations as she later did, and the Old World tropics would not have been so quickly developed. Without the European livestock, and expecially horses and mules for transport and cultivation, the American continent could not have been developed at the rate it has been." *Ibid.*, pp. 275–276.

23. Stanley Lebergott, "Labor Force and Employment, 1800–1960," in Brady (ed.), *Output, Employment and Productivity in U.S. after 1800, op. cit.*, p. 119.

tion.[24] Hybrid corn, it should be understood, is not a single strain uniformly superior in different localities. It is, rather, the outcome of a complex process of continued self-pollination together with a selection procedure which may be employed to breed a superior corn for any specific locality. Although the increase in output resulting from the use of hybrid corn varies considerably, the most generally cited figure is an increase of 20 percent in corn yields. In an important article, Griliches estimated the social rate of return over the period 1910–55 to the public and private resources committed to agricultural research which resulted in the development of hybrid corn. He estimated these returns to be of the order of 700 percent. Since Griliches was deliberately over-conservative in his calculations, this estimated rate of return may safely be regarded as a lower bound.[25]

Griliches has shown, moreover, that both the spatial and chronological diffusion of hybrid corn can be largely accounted for in terms of economic variables. The earlier and the more rapid adoption of hybrid seeds in the corn belt, and its later and slower diffusion elsewhere, can be explained in terms of profit expectations on the part of farmers and seed suppliers. The clear superiority of the hybrids over the open-pollinated varieties of corn resulted in a sweeping displacement of open-pol-

24. "Hybrid corn is the product of a controlled, systematic crossing of specially selected parental strains called 'inbred lines.' These inbred lines are developed by inbreeding, or self-pollinating, for a period of four or more years. Accompanying inbreeding is a rigid selection for the elimination of those inbreeds carrying poor heredity, and which, for one reason or another, fail to meet established standards." N.P. Neal and A.M. Strommen, "Wisconsin Corn Hybrids," Wisconsin Agricultural Experiment Station, Bulletin 476, February 1948, p. 4. As quoted in Zvi Griliches, "Hybrid Corn: An Exploration in the Economics of Technological Change," *Econometrica*, October 1957, p. 502.

25. Zvi Griliches, "Research Costs and Social Returns: Hybrid Corn and Related Innovations," *Journal of Political Economy*, October 1958, pp. 419–431.

linated corn in the corn belt in a very short period of time, with lagged as well as slower rates of adoption in the South and other more marginal areas. In Iowa, where the hybrid corn was particularly well-suited, and the shift highly profitable, it took only four years for farmers to shift from 10 to 90 percent of their corn acreage in hybrid corn. (Figure 2). On the western fringes of the corn belt, where the land was not well-adapted to growing corn, the acceptance of the hybrids was much slower—specifically, in the western portions of the Dakotas, Nebraska, and Kansas.[26]

In some very significant ways the earlier and continuing movement toward mechanization in agriculture and the more recent genetic-biological sources of productivity growth are now merging. Plant breeding raises productivity in many ways: by increasing the size and improving the quality of the plant, by developing plants which are disease-resistant, requiring a shorter growing season, etc. In addition, however, a major thrust of current plant breeding is the development of new plant varieties which lend themselves more successfully to the requirements of mechanization, particularly at the labor-intensive harvesting stage. The highly adaptable modern combine, uniting as it does the reaping and threshing operations in a single machine, now makes possible the totally mechanical harvesting of grain. Furthermore, the plants themselves are now being "redesigned," as were guns and cutlery in the nineteenth century, so that they can be produced more effectively by ma-

---

26. For an important study of a major nineteenth-century agricultural innovation, see Paul David, "The Mechanization of Reaping in the Ante-Bellum Midwest," in Henry Rosovsky (ed.), *Industrialization in Two Systems* (New York: John Wiley, 1966), pp. 3–39. David shows, by the use of a threshold function, how economic constraints regulated the timing of the introduction of the reaper on family-sized farms in the Middle West. The study derives much interest from the historical fact that the mechanical reaper had been available for twenty years before the sudden beginning of its rapid adoption after 1853.

Figure 3

Percent of Total Corn Acreage Planted with Hybrid Seed

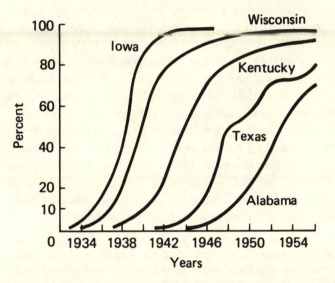

chinery.[27] Similarly, in cotton, breeding has been directed toward simplifying the mechanical picking of the crop; entirely new strains of rice have been developed which, with the great increase in fertilizer inputs, will resist lodging; sufficiently tough-skinned tomatoes (which are also uniform in size and ripen at the same time) are being successfully bred to enable them to withstand mechanical handling, and in order to facilitate mechanical harvesting, the corn in the Midwest now consists almost entirely of a specially-bred, stiff-stalked variety which will remain upright well into the fall.

The work of the plant breeder has gone beyond the limitations imposed by the range of characteristics which are found to occur within the germ plasm of any plant, and has assumed the form of genetic engineering. The breeder now possesses techniques for broadening the germ plasm base itself—for example, through chemical mutagens or irradiation.

Phenomenal results have been obtained through breakage of chromosomes and reassortment of the fragments. As an illustration, leaf rust resistance was transferred to wheat from a weedy wild relative. Close linkage of the rust-resistant gene to undesirable characters precluded its use. Through irradiation, the chromosome was broken, thereby freeing the resistant gene from the undesirable genes and providing a high type of resistance to leaf rust in wheat. Segments of rye chromosomes also have been incorporated into wheat leading to germ plasm with higher protein and rust-resistance. The vast potential of this system of breeding has been realized only to a limited degree.[28]

27. " . . . [P]lant breeders are working to adapt the plants more closely to the machine, seeking to develop varieties that will have a higher ratio of grain to straw, that will dry more evenly in the field, that will withstand more wind without shattering and that will produce more grain per acre." Clarence F. Kelly, "Mechanical Harvesting," *Scientific American*, August 1967, p. 53.

28. "Intensification of Plant Production," chap. 3 in *The World Food Problem*, A Report of the President's Science Advisory Committee, United States Government Printing Office, May 1967, vol. 2, pp. 202–203.

The long-term rise in agricultural productivity was dramatically accelerated in the years after World War II. A strong inducement to mechanization was imparted by the growing demand for labor in the non-farm sectors during the war, which raised wages and led to a large-scale movement of labor out of agriculture. Whereas in the 1920s much of the mechanization had constituted a substitution of machines for animal power as the internal combustion engine became a major supplier of traction power (see Table 6), after 1940 the main impact of mechanization was to bring about a sharp reduction in labor requirements per unit of output. This was made possible by increases in the versatility of machinery, by changes in size and design, by the use of a growing family of attachments, and by reductions in the price of machine power—e.g., higher-compression engines. The striking reduction in labor requirements is apparent in the post-World War II figures (see Table 7).

Table 6

Draft Animals and Motor Equipment on Farms, Selected
Years, 1920–1965
(Number in Thousands)

January 1	Tractors	Motor Trucks	Grain Combines	Horses & Mules	Corn Pickers	Pickup Balers
1920	246	139	4	25,700	10	n.a.
1925	549	459	. .	22,600	n.a.	n.a.
1930	920	900	61	19,100	50	n.a.
1935	1,048	890	. .	16,700	n.a.	n.a.
1940	1,567	1,047	190	14,500	110	n.a.
1945	2,354	1,490	375	12,000	168	42
1950	3,394	2,207	714	7,800	456	196
1955	4,345	2,675	980	4,300	688	448
1960	4,684	2,826	1,040	3,100	795	680
1965	4,783	3,023	910	a	690	751

a—Estimate discontinued because of insufficient information.
n.a.—Not available.

Source: *Agricultural Statistics.*

Table 7

Selected Crops: Man-Hours per Unit of Production and Related Factors, United States, Indicated Periods, 1910–66[1]

Crop and Item	1910–14	1925–29	1935–39	1945–49	1955–59	1962–66[2]
Corn for grain:						
Man-hours per acre	35.2	30.3	28.1	19.2	9.9	6.2
Yield-bushels	26.0	26.3	26.1	36.1	48.7	68.0
Man-hours per 100 bushels	135	115	108	53	20	9
Sorghum grain:						
Man-hours per acre		17.5	13.1	8.8	5.9	4.4
Yield-bushels		16.8	12.8	17.8	29.2	47.4
Man-hours per 100 bushels		104	102	49	20	9
Wheat:						
Man-hours per acre	15.2	10.5	8.8	5.7	3.8	2.9
Yield-bushels	14.4	14.1	13.2	16.9	22.3	25.9
Man-hours per 100 bushels	106	74	67	34	17	11
Hay:						
Man-hours per acre	11.9	12.0	11.3	8.4	6.0	5.3
Yield-ton	1.15	1.22	1.24	1.35	1.61	1.79
Man-hours per ton	10.3	9.8	9.1	6.2	3.7	3.0
Potatoes:						
Man-hours per acre	76.0	73.1	69.7	68.5	53.1	46.8
Yield-cwt	59.8	68.4	70.3	117.8	178.1	108.3
Man-hours per ton	25	21	20	12	6	5
Sugarbeets:						
Man-hours per acre	128	109	98	85	51	36
Yield-ton	10.6	10.9	11.6	13.6	17.4	17.3
Man-hours per ton	12.1	10.0	8.4	6.3	2.9	2.1
Cotton:						
Man-hours per acre	116	96	99	83	66	40
Yield-pounds	201	171	226	273	428	501
Man-hours per bale	276	268	309	146	74	39
Tobacco:						
Man-hours per acre[3]	356	370	415	460	475	496
Yield-pounds	816	772	886	1,176	1,541	1,958
Man-hours per 100 pounds	44	48	47	39	31	25

Soybeans:					
Man-hours per acre[3]	15.9	11.8	8.0	5.2	4.8
Yield-bushels	12.6	18.5	19.6	22.7	24.3
Man-hours per 100 bushels	126	64	41	23	20

[1]Man-hours per acre harvested, including preharvest work on acreages abandoned, grazed, and turned under.
[2]Preliminary.
[3]Per acre planted and harvested.

Source: *Agricultural Statistics*, 1967.

World War II serves also to mark a transition to substantially higher yields of output per acre, a rise which greatly exceeds anything in our earlier historical experience (see Table 7). These increases are the outcome of several factors, including the varietal improvements made possible by the growth of biological knowledge, greater use of irrigation facilities, and the shifting patterns of regional specialization as production was concentrated in areas best suited to particular crops.[29] The most important single factor, however, has been a growing utilization of chemical inputs in agriculture: herbicides and insecticides, but, far more important, reliance upon commercial fertilizers, especially synthetic nitrogenous fertilizers. The quantity of fertilizer inputs into American agriculture increased more than four times between 1940 and the mid-1960s (see Table 8). This increase in turn was induced by a drastic decline in fertilizer prices relative to product prices and the

29. On the other hand, modern machine techniques are being developed in some cases which are adapted to local conditions and terrain.

137

prices of other inputs.[30] Underlying the relative decline in the price of fertilizer were technological improvements in chemical engineering and in power production, since power is a major component in the cost of synthetic fertilizer. Here too, as in so many other areas, the shift in the materials basis of productive activity was from reliance upon organic materials to a reliance upon inorganic sources of supply.[31]

The growth in agricultural productivity has had numerous consequences, the most apparent of which has been a continued decline in the proportion of the labor force directly engaged in agriculture. But the problems of social adjustment have been further exacerbated by the specific locational impact of the new agricultural technology. For example, the decline in cotton growing in the uplands of the Old South was caused, in part, by the rapid rise and utilization of man-made fibers, a matter which will be examined shortly. In addition, however, the introduction of the mechanical cotton picker, which began in the 1920s, hastened the decline of the crop in this particular region. Since the mechanical cotton picker works much more effectively on a flat terrain than on a hilly one, this innovation (together with the increased use of liquid nitrogenous fertilizers) played an important role in shifting the cultivation of the

30. The motivation to raise output per acre has also, of course, been strengthened by government programs involving acreage restrictions. For an analysis of fertilizer price changes relative to the prices of farm products and other inputs, and of the contribution of technological change to the relative decline in fertilizer prices, see G. S. Sahota, "The Sources of Measured Productivity Growth: U.S. Fertilizer Mineral Industries, 1936–1960," *Review of Economics and Statistics*, May 1966, pp. 193–204.

31. Justus von Liebig's great treatise on agricultural chemistry, *Organic Chemistry in its Relations to Agriculture and Physiology*, appeared in German and English in 1840. Modern techniques of commercial fertilizers, involving the fixation of atmospheric nitrogen, were the eventual but logical outcome of the work initiated by von Liebig.

crop out of its traditional region and into the broad, flat, previously barren regions of west Texas, Arizona, and California.

The resulting outmigration of Negro labor from the rural economy of the old Confederacy as a result of the new technology is a basic fact underlying the growth of American urban ghettos in recent years.[32] Thus, there is a direct causal relationship between the decline of an old social system in the South and the growing evidence of poverty in the metropolitan north. As Kain and Persky have recently asserted:

It is our contention that the migration streams originating in the rural South form the crucial link in a system of poverty; a system nurtured by the inability or unwillingness of rural communities to adequately prepare their children for the complexities of modern life; a system brought to fruition in the metropolitan area too crowded and too shortsighted to rectify these mistakes. While much of this argument appears to be obvious for the southern Negro migrant, it is important to realize that a similar causal chain explains substantial amounts of metropolitan white poverty. The Appalachian South plays a role for white urban poverty (especially in the North Central region) similar to that which the Core South plays vis-à-vis the metropolitan ghetto. While the southern white does not come up against the same obstacles of discrimination that meet the southern Negro, he does suffer from similar, if not as extreme, educational and vocational handicaps. . . . [S]outhern-born white and Negro migrants are ill prepared for life in the metropolitan North. This implies that they are different from other residents of northern metropolitan areas. The southern-born migrant to the North is clearly and identifiably different if he is Negro. As we discuss more fully below, this fact is in itself of considerable importance given the problems created by the rapid growth of Negro ghettos in northern cities. However, our analysis implies that the migrants are different in other less visible ways as well. In particu-

---

32. The technological factors creating the push out of southern agriculture are well treated in James H. Street, *The New Revolution in the Cotton Economy* (Chapel Hill, N.C.: University of North Carolina Press, 1957), Part III.

Technology and American Economic Growth

Table 8

Commercial Fertilizers—Quantities Consumed and Average
Primary Plant Nutrient Content (Thousands of Tons)

Year	Quantity	Percent		
		Nitrogen	Phosphoric-oxide	Potash
1940	8,556	4.9	10.7	5.1
1950	20,345	6.1	10.4	6.8
1955	21,404	9.0	10.5	8.8
1960	24,374	12.4	10.9	8.9
1965	33,071	16.1	11.8	9.7
1966 (prel.)	35,731	16.9	12.1	10.1

Source: *Statistical Abstract of the U.S.*, 1968.

lar, they are likely to be poorly educated, have high levels of unemployment and low incomes, and place disproportionate demands on welfare and public services.[33]

The broad parallels between the impact of the knowledge revolution in materials and in agriculture are wide-ranging in their significance. In both areas highly developed scientific disciplines now make it possible to go far beyond the much more passive adaptations to natural surroundings to which we have previously been restricted. In both agriculture and the world of industrial material inputs it is now possible to initiate new things—such as hybrids and seed varietals in agriculture and new alloys and synthetic polymers in materials. We are no longer confined to establishing, through rather haphazard empirical techniques, which corn will grow best in a particular environment, or which iron ore will work most successfully

33. John F. Kain and Joseph J. Persky, "The North's Stake in Southern Rural Poverty," in *Rural Poverty in the United States: A Report by the President's National Advisory Commission on Rural Poverty*, Washington, D.C., May 1968, chap. 17, pp. 291–294.

with a given coal supply. Now it is possible, in a serious sense, to improve upon nature. We can exploit our knowledge of genetics and biochemistry in agriculture and of molecular architecture in materials to create new seeds and new synthetic materials with optimum characteristics in satisfying human requirements.

A major thrust of twentieth-century technology as it has been based upon the knowledge revolution has been to reduce dependence upon specific natural resource inputs. In some respects this is not a new phenomenon. After all, industrial technology since the seventeenth and eighteenth centuries has been preoccupied with liberating productive enterprise from severe constraints imposed by dependence upon organic sources: food products, wood for fuel and construction, animal energy, plant and animal fibers and materials (wool, leather, cotton, silk) for clothing and textile products generally. The classic Industrial Revolution in Britain substituted cheap coal for wood as a source of fuel and power and cheap and abundant iron for vanishing timber resources. The great achievements of the Industrial Revolution, precise and reliable machinery, railroads, large-span bridges, great iron ships, and innumerable feats of engineering virtuosity, would all have been impossible in the absence of cheap iron.

The more recent materials revolution may be regarded as carrying this liberation process to an entirely new level. Not only are metals being produced and alloyed in ways which make them much more "finely tuned" to specific human purposes (e.g., the precisely articulated needs of the space program)[34] but

---

34. Thus, the nose-cones of re-entry vehicles are plastic materials which are (1) light, (2) resistant to mechanical shock, (3) possess a high degree of thermal stability, (4) thermally non-conductive, and (5) easy to fabricate.

entirely new products are being synthesized which bear only the remotest relation to materials occurring in nature.[35]

Although it is somewhat less obvious, the current biological revolution in agriculture is part of the same process of reducing human dependence upon the raw facts of nature, more particularly upon its organic products. Although food products continue to be grown on land (a dependence which may some day be terminated by hydroponics), the productive contribution of land relative to other inputs has been declining. One way of looking at the impact of technological change in agriculture over the past century is to say that a growing portion of farm output is produced by nonfarm inputs and a smaller proportion is attributable to the input of land itself. This is measurable by looking at the ratio of purchased inputs to total agricultural output, a ratio which has been rising for several decades. In contrast to the long term trend toward the mechanization of American agriculture, the major effect of which was and continues to be labor-saving, the effect of the growth in the economically-relevant stock of biological knowledge in recent decades has been to impart a pronounced land-saving bias to technological change.[36]

35. Although some synthetic materials have counterparts in nature after which they are modeled—rubber, leather, fibers, fur—synthetic resins have no such counterparts and cannot be identified with particular materials.

36. The substitution of the tractor for the horse was, of course, a highly land-saving innovation. If horses rather than tractors were required to provide all the traction power currently employed on American farms, a staggering quantity of acreage would be required to keep them in oats. "In 1920, approximately 90 million acres of cropland were used to feed horses and mules on farms, and some unknown additional acreage produced feed for similar animals off farms. By 1960, less than 10 million acres were used for this purpose. Thus, the output of one-fourth or more of all the cropland in the United States was shifted . . . to the production of farm products for human consumption. . . ." Dale E. Hathaway, *Government and Agriculture* (New York: The Macmillan Company, 1963), p. 99.

The American farmer is now much less self-reliant than he was one hundred years ago, when he in fact produced his own power sources (draft animals) as well as their fuel (oats, hay, etc.), in addition to providing many of his own consumer goods and services, including his food (which he now purchases, in a highly processed state, like urban residents, by driving to a nearby supermarket.[37]) Furthermore, whereas his son could adequately equip himself for the life of a farmer through the on-the-job training he received at his father's side, the sophisticated skills and decisions required of modern farmers make a university education highly desirable. In these respects, the American farmer has shared in the growing reliance upon specialist suppliers of materials, goods and services which has become so characteristic of the rest of the economy, including the household sector. He is now dependent in his operations upon purchases from a long chain of materials suppliers: commercial fertilizer, feed for livestock, seeds and insecticides, as well as machinery and fuel.[38] (Indeed, reductions in transport costs, together with the growth of commercial suppliers of mixed

37. An index number (1957–59 = 100) of the volume of farm output which was retained for on-farm consumption declined from 191 in 1940 to 46 in 1968. U.S. Dept. of Agriculture, Economic Research Service, *Farm Income Situation*, July 1969, Table 2.

38. In 1968 American farmers spent $24.95 billion on the purchase of farm inputs. The breakdown was as follows:

Feed	$6,474,000,000
Livestock	3,628,000,000
Seed	668,000,000
Fertilizer and Lime	2,095,000,000
Repair and operation of capital items (primarily machinery)	4,614,000,000
Hired labor	3,042,000,000
Miscellaneous purchases	4,430,000,000

Source: U.S. Dept. of Agriculture, Economic Research Service, *Farm Income Situation*, July 1969, Table 13H.

feeds and the increasingly specialized knowledge required in livestock production, are bringing about a growing locational as well as managerial separation between crop and livestock production.) And moreover, he utilizes knowledge inputs which are made available to him through a complex network including the United States Department of Agriculture, land-grant colleges, agricultural experiment stations, government meteorologists, seed, equipment, and commercial fertilizer producers, and county agents. Although the family farm still shows a sturdy persistence as a producing unit, it is now hopelessly inadequate for the acquisition and diffusion of knowledge.

This growing skill in offsetting the scarcity of particular natural resources by exploiting alternative, more abundant sources, by innovations which reduce resource requirements per unit of output, and by the development of synthetic materials has falsified the dire, dismal predictions of classical economics.[39] Ricardo and Malthus saw the future prospects for an industrial society such as England as being dominated by the inability to offset the resource constraints imposed by the limited supply of land.[40] Their intense interest in foreign trade of course followed from this basic vision. But we now see that technological change

39. Mention should also be made here of the increasing skill at exploiting low-concentrate, "inferior" raw materials. Low grade mineral deposits such as shale oil and taconite iron ore are available domestically in enormous quantity and will become increasingly practical as the supplies of more abundant, high quality deposits are exhausted and as technological mastery of their exploitation grows. The utilization of many of these low quality sources, such as that of bauxite, is highly sensitive to fuel and power costs, so that innovations which reduce these costs will also give a strong impetus to their exploitation. Furthermore, we have also learned how to make aluminum from clays of which the country possesses an immense supply, thereby freeing aluminum entirely from its dependence upon bauxite reserves.

40. Similarly, the distinguished English economist W. S. Jevons, in his book *The Coal Question*, published in 1865, warned of the impending decline of British industry due to the inevitably rising costs of coal extraction.

has provided another, highly effective set of possibilities for reducing the dependence of an expanding industrial society upon its natural resource inputs. Resources in their unprocessed state have, in fact, demonstrably been playing a role of diminishing importance. If we express the value of resource output as a percentage of GNP, this figure has been declining since 1870, the earliest date for which figures are available. The resource-GNP ratio was 36 percent in 1870, 27 percent in 1900, 17 percent in 1930, and 12 percent in 1954[41] (see Table 9).

Thus, Godwin was surely better equipped as a prognosticator than Malthus when, in his debate with the latter, he committed to paper the following remarkably prescient statement:

Of all the sciences, natural or mechanical, which within the last half century have proceeded with such gigantic strides, chemistry is that which has advanced the most rapidly. All the substances that nature presents, all that proceeds from earth or air, is analyzed by us into its original elements. Thus we have discovered, or may discover, precisely what it is that nourishes the human body. And it is surely no great stretch of the faculty of anticipation, to say, that whatever man can

41. The ratio, of course, is a reflection of a variety of factors. As consumers' incomes rise they shift their expenditures to goods and services where raw material costs are less important than in a budget dominated by food products. Furthermore, even in the case of food products, their final prices now incorporate a much larger proportion of processing, fabrication, packaging, transportation, and distribution costs than was the case in the nineteenth century. Therefore, even in the case of food purchases, a smaller fraction of each dollar of expenditure represents the cost of purchasing raw materials.

In view of the concern of the classical economists with growing resource scarcity and the consequent rise in the share of the national income going to rent receivers, it is worth pointing out that the share of rents in the national income of the United Kingdom declined from an estimated 13.7% in the 1860s to 4.9% in the 1950s. P. Deane and W. A. Cole, *British Economic Growth 1688–1959* (Cambridge: Cambridge University Press, 1962), p. 247. To be sure, there are serious conceptual problems in comparing the definition of rent used by Deane and Cole with the usage of the classical economists. Nevertheless, it is unmistakably clear that the distribution of income has not been dominated by an inexorably rising rental share in the national income.

Table 9

Output of Resources as a Percent of GNP
(1954 Prices)

	All Resources	Agriculture	Timber Products	Minerals
1870	36	27	4.0	1.5
1880	32	25	3.7	2.0
1890	29	21	3.9	2.8
1900	27	19	3.9	3.4
1910	22	15	2.8	4.2
1920	21	14	2.0	4.9
1930	17	11	1.2	4.3
1940	16	10	1.0	4.1
1950	13	8	.77	3.6
1954	12	8	.69	3.3

Source: Joseph Fisher and Edward Boorstein, *The Adequacy of Resources for Economic Growth in the United States,* Study Paper No. 13, Prepared in Connection with the Study of Employment, Growth, and Price Levels, 86th Congress, December 16, 1959, p. 43.

decompose, man will be able to compound. The food that nourishes us, is composed of certain elements; and wherever these elements can be found, human art will hereafter discover the power of reducing them into a state capable of affording corporeal sustenance. No good reason can be assigned, why that which produces animal nourishment, must have previously passed through a process of animal or vegetable life. And, if a certain infusion of attractive exterior qualities is held necessary to allure us to our food, there is no reason to suppose that the most agreeable colours and scents and flavours may not be imparted to it, at a very small expense of vegetable substance. Thus it appears that, wherever earth, and water, and the other original chemical substances may be found, there human art may hereafter produce nourishment: and thus we are presented with a real infinite series of increase of the means of subsistence, to match Mr. Malthus's geometrical ratio for the multiplication of mankind. . . . [42]

42. William Godwin, *Of Population* (London, 1820), pp. 499–501.

Modern technology may now be said to have displaced the primacy of natural resources in determining a country's growth prospects. Obviously this does not mean that natural resources are unimportant. But it does mean that the human agent is vastly more powerful and resourceful than, say, a hundred years ago, and this technological mastery has immensely expanded the options available to him. Nevertheless, resource endowment continues to play a major role in determining the relative cost of alternative actions. Maine will doubtless continue to resist the temptation to grow bananas in hothouses; the recent growth of the synthetic fiber industry in the South was heavily influenced by its dependence for its basic raw materials upon the petrochemical plants of the Southwest; and the location of steel mills continues to be influenced by the desire to minimize the cost of transporting their bulky input requirements.[43] However, the number of alternative materials now available as substitutes for steel in different uses is very great, and steel itself may, as a result, be on the way to becoming a declining industry.[44]

43. The fact that mineral deposits are generally less widely diffused spatially than agricultural and forestry resources is, by itself, a powerful factor in according locational advantages to specific areas. Improvements in transportation technology, on the other hand, tend to reduce the size of these advantages.

44. Some interesting insights into the difficulties of introducing new products into a centrally managed economy were provided by Premier Khrushchev in 1962. In his report to the Central Committee of the Soviet Communist Party in November 1962, Mr. Khrushchev lambasted the State Planning Committee for its hesitancy with respect to the introduction of plastics: "Had planning and economic organs studied economic problems more profoundly they should have determined when and in what quantities ferrous and nonferrous metals and other materials should be replaced by synthetic materials, and developed their production in every way. Unfortunately, economic and planning organs do not take sufficient account of the achievements of science and technology, do not use these achievements for the accelerated development of those categories of production and branches which are economically the most advantageous and promising. . . .

The point here is one of great general importance. By increasing the number of good substitutes for any input, the growth in knowledge is adding a new and effective form to the competitive process, a form which is not adequately perceived by the conventional examination of market structures and industry concentration ratios. A direct consequence of the knowledge revolution, a revolution whose immediate consequence is to widen the range of substitute inputs and outputs, is to make the economy more effectively competitive. It is, for example, impossible to appreciate the nature of competitive forces with respect to steel by focusing solely upon the steel industry, where there appears to be abundant evidence of concentration and market power. The competition which increasingly matters for the steel producers is not the behavior of other firms in the steel industry but the behavior of a whole range of firms producing products which are in most respects quite unlike steel but which are highly effective substitutes for steel in particular uses.[45] Aluminum has successfully displaced steel in many of its traditional markets, especially where lightness and resistance to corrosion are highly desired, and so have magnesium and titanium on a smaller scale. (All three metals, of course, have been important in the development of modern jet

"Production of steel is, so to speak, a well-worn road with deep tracks, and here even a blind horse will not swerve because the wheels will break. A material has appeared which is superior to steel and cheaper, but they still shout: Steel! Steel! If we had only fulfilled the plan for the smelting of steel but overfulfilled it for polyethylene we would have done better and would be much richer. But this is hard to do because there are people in the State Planning Committee who stop those who sensibly want to change the steel production targets in favour of synthetic materials." As quoted in C. Freeman, "The Plastics Industry: A Comparative Study of Research and Innovation," *National Institute Economic Review*, November 1963, pp. 48–49.

45. The steel industry has also been deeply affected by some "internal" developments such as the increasing prominence of steel alloys and the reuse of scrap steel.

aircraft.) Structural concrete has become a formidable competitor to steel for many construction purposes, especially as the performance characteristics of such concrete have been greatly improved. There is now abundant visual evidence of this substitution in American cities. Increasingly tough and durable plastics are being developed, and are even being introduced into such uses as gears and bearings, and as the major plastics groups continue to decline in price they too have come to constitute a growing competitor to steel, as well as to many other materials.[46] Polyethylene pipe, for example, has largely displaced stainless steel pipe in certain corrosive applications.[47]

This new form of the competitive mechanism exerts itself in many directions, such as to make an orderly approach to the subject on the basis of conventional definitions of industrial boundaries an essentially meaningless exercise.[48] Aluminum

46. Although the machine tool industry has been an insignificant user of steel, the particular *properties* of steel and steel alloys employed in metal-cutting tools have long been of vital importance in determining the efficiency of machine tools, because these properties establish the maximum speeds at which the machines can perform. Here too, it is interesting to note, steel tools have been giving way to tools made of new materials such as cemented carbide or ceramics. At the same time, machine tools as a way of shaping metals are beginning to be displaced by entirely different techniques of metal forming: metal stamping, precision forging, casting, explosive forming, etc.

47. The importance throughout the entire manufacturing sector of "competition by innovation" has recently been employed to account for the composition of American manufacturing exports—a composition which appeared to be at variance with traditional comparative cost theory. See the highly suggestive article by Raymond Vernon, "International Investments and International Trade in the Product Cycle," *Quarterly Journal of Economics,* May 1966, pp. 190–207.

48. "Any consideration of the textile industry would be artificial which did not include the chemical, plastics, and paper industries. Consideration of the machine tool industry now must take into account the aerospace, precision casting, forging, and plastics forming industries. These industries are now complex mixtures of companies from a variety of SIC categories, some functioning as suppliers to the traditional industry, some competing with it for end-use functions and markets. 'The industry' can no longer be defined as a set of

has replaced steel in many uses, but it has also, due to its comparative cheapness and lightness, been accepted as a substitute for copper in the long-distance transmission of electricity. Aluminum, together with plastics, has displaced wood in many of its former uses, as in construction and in packaging.[49] Plastics, in turn, in different contexts have substituted for natural fibers, wood, rubber, leather, glass, and many metals.

The growing importance of man-made materials and the relative (and in some cases absolute) decline in the older, more traditional materials is evident in Table 10 which shows production figures for a variety of materials over a recent decade. The phenomenal rise of synthetic materials from a longer time perspective may be indicated by the fact that, between 1931 and 1966, output of plastics grew at an annual rate of almost 17 percent. In the latter year more than 13,500,000,000 pounds of plastics were produced with a sales value in excess of $2,700,-000,000.

Greater mastery over the realm of materials makes possible a continuous substitution and exploitation of more abundant

companies who share certain methods of production and product-properties; it must be defined as a set of companies, interconnected as suppliers and market, committed to diverse processes and products, but overlapping in the end-use functions they fill. We can talk about the 'shelter' industry and the 'materials forming' industry, but we cannot make the assumptions of coherence, similarity and uniformity of view which we could formerly make in speaking of 'builders' or 'machine tool manufacturers.' Similarly, companies are coming to be less devoted to a single family of products and manufacturing methods, and more a diverse conglomerate of manufacturing enterprises, stationed around a central staff and bank, and to some extent overlapping in the markets and functions they serve." Arthur D. Little, Inc., *Patterns and Problems of Technical Innovation in American Industry,* Report to National Science Foundation, U.S. Dept. of Commerce, Washington, D.C., 1963, p. 181.

49. Technical change has also brought about methods which economize upon wood requirements without the substitution of competitive materials, or which substitute cheaper woods for more expensive woods—for example, plywood and wood veneers.

Table 10

Output of Selected Materials, 1956–1966

	1956	1966	Percent Change
Plastics[1]	3,977	13,585	+240
Rubber, synthetic[1]	2,420	4,414	+ 82.5
Aluminum[2]	1,697	2,968	+ 77
Alloy steels[2]	10,338	15,369	+ 49
Copper[2]	1,443	1,711	+ 18.6
Steel[2]	115,216	134,101	+ 16.4
Zinc[2]	984	1,025	+ 4.2
Rubber, natural[1]	1,260	1,241	− 1.6
Lumber[3]	38,629	36,128	− 6.3

[1]Millions of pounds.
[2]Thousands of short tons.
[3]Millions of board feet.

Source: U.S. Department of Commerce, *Business Statistics*, 1967.

materials for scarcer ones. In order to understand this process, however, we must think of the specific properties for which a material is desired in a particular use and not the *combination* of characteristics which it possesses in its natural, unprocessed state. The point has been well expressed by Anthony Scott:

[T]he market does not eagerly desire a specific element or compound for long. Demand for minerals is *derived* from demand for certain final goods and services. Therefore, certain properties must be obtainable from the raw materials from which such services and types of final goods are produced. Man's hunt for minerals must properly be viewed as a hunt for economical sources of these properties (strength, colour, porosity, conductivity, magnetism, texture, size, durability, elasticity, flavour, and so on). For example, there is no demand for "tin," but for something to make copper harder or iron corrosion-free. No one substitute for tin has been found, but each of the functions performed by tin can now be performed in other ways. Tin's hardening of copper (as in bronze) has been supplanted by the use of other metals. Food need no longer be packed in tin cans. Hence the immense capital investment that society might have been forced to undertake to satisfy its former needs for tin from the minute, low-grade quantities to be found in many parts of the world have been replaced by simpler investments in obtaining other materials. Chief of of the replacements for tin is glass, made from apparently unlimited quantities of sand and with little more energy than is needed to bring metallic tin to the user. Lead and mercury are being bypassed in similar fashion; zinc and copper may be next.[50]

The rise of synthetic materials in the form of man-made fibers for use in textiles has now reached the point where these new materials are surpassing the traditional natural fibers, especially cotton. In recent years synthetic fibers have been introduced in clothing, carpeting, drapery and upholstery fabrics, and home furnishings (sheets, pillowcases, bedspreads, tablecloths). Their great popularity, especially in clothing, is attributable to special characteristics, many of which are achieved by blending (including blending with natural fibers), such as greater strength, ease of laundering, lightness, crease retention, fast drying, etc.[51] In the United States in 1968, the quantity, by weight, of synthetic fibers actually surpassed that of natural fibers for the first

50. Anthony Scott, "The Development of the Extractive Industries," *Canadian Journal of Economics and Political Science*, February 1962, pp. 80–81.

51. This follows from the outstanding properties of individual fibers. Thus:

Fiber	Outstanding Property
Nylon	Abrasion resistance
Orlon	High bulk
Dacron	Great resilience
Acrilan	Bulking power, dyeing, and resistance to pilling
Dynel	Resistance to burning.

Arthur D. Little, Inc., *Patterns and Problems of Technical Innovation in American Industry, op. cit.*, p. 32.

time.[52] The new materials have had a great effect in revitalizing the textile industry in recent years.

This new form of the competitive process may serve also to energize other old, established industries. This is a form of competition about which conventional economic theory has had relatively little to say. There are numerous historical instances where an outside threat to a well-established industry has had a potent effect, and has galvanized its members into action far surpassing the impact of competition among its members. The sailing ship, for example, was subjected to important improvements in design and construction after the advent of the steamship. More recently, the major steel producers, who for long did not appear very actively involved with intraindustry competition, seem to have responded with both energy and imagination to interindustry competition. The encroachment of aluminum upon the traditional domain of steel seems to have been responsible for the establishment of new research laboratories and an awakening of interest in product engineering. These efforts have met with at least partial success.[53]

Interindustry competition has also been particularly important among different forms of fuel—wood, coal, oil, natural gas

52. See Table 11.
53. Writing of these efforts on the part of the steel industry, an observer recently commented: "Toward recovery of the substantial portion of the container industry lost to light weight, easy formability and corrosion resistance of aluminum, they have reduced by two-thirds the thickness of strip rolled for cans and are looking for ways to eliminate the expensive tin and tinning process. In the construction industry, steelmakers turned back a challenge from aluminum alloys for short-span highway bridges, but they had to share this victory with reinforced concrete. Conversely, it appears that steel has lost the skyscraper curtain-wall market. Here the properties desired are lightness, appearance and constancy of surface. Aluminum, anodized to various colors and finishes, has proved more desirable than even stainless steel and much less expensive." W. O. Alexander, "The Competition of Materials," *Scientific American*, September 1967, p. 264.

Table 11

Mill Consumption of Natural and Man-Made Fibers
(Millions of Pounds)

Year	Natural Fibers			Synthetic Fibers		
	Cotton	Wool	Total	Rayons & Acetate	Other	Total
1930	2,617	263	2,880	119		119
1935	2,755	418	3,173	274		274
1940	3,959	408	4,367	494	4	498
1945	4,516	645	5,161	795	50	845
1950	4,683	635	5,318	1,375	144	1,519
1955	4,382	414	4,796	1,455	448	1,903
1960	4,191	411	4,602	1,082	796	1,878
1963	4,040	412	4,452	1,471	1,317	2,788
1964	4,244	357	4,601	1,556	1,618	3,174
1965	4,477	387	4,864	1,593	2,031	3,624
1966	4,631	370	5,001	1,623	2,379	4,002
1967	4,423	313	4,736	1,520	2,723	4,243
1968 (prel.)	4,146	330	4,476	1,713	3,588	5,301

Source: *Statistical Abstract of the U.S.*, 1968 and 1969.

—and among different forms of transportation. It is not even inconceivable that such competition may revive portions of the railroad industry which have long been regarded as moribund.[54] In any case it has certainly been true that possible

54. "The pressure of competition from natural gas, from the potential of the coal pipeline, and from nuclear energy, combined with a changed attitude of the regulatory authorities, has moved railroads to introduce wholly new handling arrangements with a minimum of new technology. Some of the attendant rate reductions have been spectacular. One of the earliest led to the closing in 1963 of the only existing coal pipeline in the United States. . . . The change in transportation methods is epitomized by the unit train, whose hallmark is specialization, in terms of commodity carried, route traveled, and equipment. Specifically designed trains, that in the extreme instance are hardly ever uncoupled, are shuttled back and forth between mine and consumer—currently for the most part electric power plants, but in the future perhaps many other

monopolistic restrictions in the railroads did not have the deleterious consequences which they might have had because of competition from a succession of new forms of transport and carriers—trucks, planes, automobiles and pipelines.[55]

The importance of interindustry competition is part of the reason, at least, why it has been so difficult to establish systematic relationships between market structure and inventive activity. Generalizations have proven to be very difficult to make. As Griliches has pointed out:

Whatever evidence we have . . . points to no particular relationship between monopoly, oligopoly, or competition and inventive activity. Neither the empirical evidence nor the theoretical discussion has established the presumption of a correlation between the degree of market control and the rate of inventive activity. Even if there were

consumers. The trains are emptied by rotating the cars around their longitudinal axes or by extra-rapid bottom dumping, and are equipped with various other speed-up devices for loading and unloading. High capital utilization is achieved and costs are reduced." Landsberg and Schurr, *op. cit.*, pp. 86–88.

55. It should also be emphasized that substitution among different consumer goods or services mitigates the exercise of market power just as does a widening of the range of substitutes among inputs. Whether dealing with inputs or outputs, a widening of the chain of substitutes enlarges the options open to the buyer and thereby reduces the potential exercise of power on the part of the seller. The effectiveness of these forces depends upon the cost of the alternatives and whether they are good or poor substitutes for the purpose in hand. But it should be remembered that substitution in the economic sense need not require a high degree of physical similarity. As Barnett and Morse have stated: "In the fuel area . . . consumers have choices among bituminous coal, anthracite coal, manufactured gas, natural gas, fuel oil, and electricity. Any onset of relative scarcity in one fuel would swing consumers to the less scarce substitutes. Fuel substitution may also be brought about through increased use of such commodities as storm windows, insulation, sweaters, and thermostats." And also: " . . . [B]roadcasting may be substituted for newsprint; sedentary vacations for peripatetic ones; public transportation for operation of private cars; wintering in Florida, or emigration to southern California, for fuel." Harold Barnett and Chandler Morse, *Scarcity and Growth* (Baltimore, Md.: The Johns Hopkins Press, 1963), pp. 130–131.

some relationship between the two (positive or negative), it could at best have only a second order effect. It would be quite inefficient, I believe, to try to affect the rate of inventive activity in the U.S. by manipulating the antitrust laws.[56]

Clearly, when we become involved in the complexities of modern technology, interindustry relationships become increasingly important. Some aspects of these relationships have, of course, been strongly illuminated by the whole input-output approach to the structure of the economy which has been developed by Wassily Leontief and his students. The point which is emphasized here is different, although related. That is to say, in addition to interindustry competition, technological progress in any sector of the economy is increasingly dependent upon developments *outside* that sector. The problems arising in one sector are resolved by resources and technical skills which reside in another sector. Earlier we examined this process in the nineteenth century and saw how the machine tool industry became the locus of mechanical skills and expertise which were exploited in the development of a new and improved technology for an ever-widening range of industries—not the least of which was agriculture.[57] In the twentieth century we have been witnessing a shift in the sources of technological change away from the mechanical and toward technologies based upon chemistry, electronics, and biology. This dependence upon science-based inputs from outside the industry concerned is by no means unique to the twentieth century, but it has as-

56. Griliches, in *The Rate and Direction of Inventive Activity, op. cit.*, p. 353.
57. Just as metallurgy is giving way to materials science, so the machine tool industry seems on the way to becoming the materials-forming industry as new techniques are developed which form metals (or other materials) without removing them—precision casting and forging, which require little or no removal of metal, greater reliance upon metal stamping rather than machining, increasing use of plastics which are shaped by other means, etc.

sumed a role of far greater importance than in any earlier period.[58]

THE CASE OF ENERGY

A basic fact about a modern industrial economy is that it utilizes enormous amounts of mineral-derived energy in the manufacture and transportation of goods and in the running of its domestic households. An index of energy consumed from mineral, hydropower, and fuelwood sources in the American economy quadrupled between 1850 and 1900 and more than quadrupled again between 1900 and 1955.[59] It is easy to forget

58. It is therefore difficult to understand why the otherwise valuable A. D. Little study, *Patterns and Problems of Technical Innovation in American Industry*, referred to earlier, treats what it describes as "innovation by invasion" in machine tools, building, and textiles as if it were a distinctively novel, modern phenomenon. Landes has recently emphasized the contribution of the chemicals industry to the expansion of textile output during the classic years of the British Industrial Revolution. "We are accustomed today to look on the chemical manufacture as a giant, partly because of its success in creating wondrous new materials like nylon or plastics, partly because of the 'miracle' drugs that pour out of its laboratories in an endless stream; we are less aware of the enormous output of what is generally known as the heavy chemical industry, which is concerned with those inorganic agents, acid and alkali, used in the production of other commodities.

"Yet the derivative character of this growth in our period in no way diminishes its importance. The transformation of the textile manufacture, whose requirements of detergents, bleaches, and mordants were growing at the same pace as output, would have been impossible without a corresponding transformation of chemical technology. There was not enough cheap meadowland or sour milk in all the British Isles to whiten the cloth of Lancashire once the water frame and mule replaced the spinning wheel; and it would have taken undreamed-of quantities of human urine to cut the grease of the raw wool consumed by the mills of the West Riding." Landes, *The Unbound Prometheus, op. cit.*, p. 108.

59. Schurr and Netschert, *Energy in the American Economy 1850–1975, op. cit.*, p. 39. In per capita terms, energy consumption in 1955 was almost 2½ times its level in 1900. *Ibid.*, p. 15.

how recent a phenomenon this dependence upon mineral sources is. Yet in 1850 mineral fuels supplied less than 10 percent whereas wood supplied more than 90 percent of all fuel-based energy (see Table 12). The other energy sources were waterpower, windpower and, of course, animal power and manpower.[60] Because of an abundance of forest resources and waterpower as well as the trans-Appalachian location of her major coal deposits, the United States proceeded much farther along the road to industrialization than had Great Britain without extensive reliance upon coal as an energy source. In 1850, most of the power employed in manufacturing was supplied by water. Although this proportion was declining, even as late as 1869, as we saw earlier, water power accounted for 48.2 percent of primary power capacity in manufacturing.[61] In the second half of the nineteenth century, however, changes in relative costs as well as technological changes favoring the use of mineral resources in the manufacture of iron and steel and the production of steam power brought about a rapid shift to coal. In the last decades of the nineteenth century steam power relying upon coal grew to the peak of its influence and in 1899 steam power accounted for over 80 percent of primary power capacity in manufacturing whereas waterpower accounted for less than 15 percent.[62] Moreover, among material sources of energy, coal had largely displaced wood by the early years of the twentieth century—from its position of overwhelming dominance in 1850 wood declined to less than 10 percent in

60. One rough calculation suggests that the power generated by falling waterpower and windpower in 1850 was the equivalent of the mechanical energy which could have been produced at the time by 19 million tons of coal. *Ibid.*, pp. 48–49.
61. Fenichel, "Growth and Diffusion of Power in Manufacturing, 1838–1919," *op. cit.*
62. Fenichel, *op. cit.*, p. 469.

Table 12

Specific Energy Sources as Percentages of Aggregate Energy Consumption, Five-Year Intervals, 1850–1955

(Measured in Btu's)

Year	Bituminous coal (1)	Anthracite (2)	Total coal (3)	Oil (4)	Natural gas (5)	Natural gas liquids (6)	Total liquids and gaseous fuels (7)	Total mineral fuels (8)	Hydro-power (9)	Mineral fuels and hydro-power (10)	Fuel wood (11)
1850	4.7%	4.6%	9.3%					9.3%			90.7%
1855	7.3	7.7	15.0					15.0			85.0
1860	7.7	8.7	16.4	.1%	n.a.		n.a.	16.5			83.5
1865	9.6	8.9	18.5	.3	n.a.		n.a.	18.8			81.2
1870	13.8	12.7	26.5	.3	n.a.		n.a.	26.8			73.2
1875	19.9	13.4	33.3	.3	n.a.		n.a.	33.6			66.4
1880	26.7	14.3	41.1	1.9	n.a.		1.9%	43.0			57.0
1885	33.4	16.9	50.3	.7	1.5%		2.2	52.5			47.5
1890	41.4	16.5	57.9	2.2	3.7		5.9	63.8	.3%	64.1%	35.9
1895	45.8	18.8	64.6	2.2	1.9		4.1	68.7	1.2	69.9	30.1
1900	56.6	14.7	71.4	2.4	2.6		5.0	76.4	2.6	79.0	21.0
1905	61.2	14.5	75.7	4.6	2.8		7.4	83.1	2.9	86.1	13.9
1910	64.3	12.4	76.8	6.1	3.3		9.3	86.1	3.3	89.3	10.7
1915	62.7	12.2	74.8	7.9	3.8		11.8	86.6	3.9	90.5	9.5
1920	62.3	10.2	72.5	12.3	3.8	.2%	16.3	88.8	3.6	92.5	7.5
1925	58.4	7.3	65.6	18.5	5.3	.6	24.4	90.0	3.1	93.2	6.8
1930	50.3	7.3	57.5	23.8	8.1	1.0	33.0	90.6	3.3	93.9	6.1
1935	45.6	6.3	52.0	26.9	9.4	0.9	37.1	89.1	4.1	93.2	6.8
1940	44.7	4.9	49.7	29.6	10.6	1.1	41.3	91.0	3.6	94.6	5.4
1945	44.8	4.0	48.8	29.4	11.8	1.5	42.8	91.6	4.5	96.1	3.9
1950	33.9	2.9	36.8	36.2	17.0	2.2	55.4	92.1	4.6	96.7	3.3
1955	27.2	1.5	28.7	40.0	22.1	2.9	65.0	93.7	3.7	97.4	2.6

n.a. Not available.

Source: Sam H. Schurr and Bruce C. Netschert, *Energy in the American Economy, 1850–1955* (Baltimore, Md.: The Johns Hopkins Press, 1960), p. 36. Reprinted by permission of the publisher.

1915 whereas coal sources accounted for three-quarters (Table 12). Subsequent decades are largely the story of the declining importance of coal—a decline in which dieselization[63] in transportation and the loss of household markets played major roles —and the rise of liquid and gaseous fuels[64] (Table 12). In contrast to the prolonged dominance of coal in other industrial countries, the supremacy of coal as an energy source was relatively short. As Table 12 shows, coal accounted for over one half of energy sources only for the period between 1885 and 1940.

Superimposed upon the expansion and changing composition of the primary sources of power is the growth of electrification, a process which has so many ramifications for twentieth-century technology as to defy any brief summary. Purely within the context of a discussion of the uses of energy, however, the electric motor represents an extraordinarily versatile technological innovation which made it possible to "package" and deliver

63. Locomotives in Service:

	Steam	Diesel
1930	59,406	77
1940	42,410	967
1945	41,018	4,301
1950	26,680	15,396
1955	6,266	26,563
1960	374	29,898
1965	89	29,552

Source: *Historical Statistics of U.S.*, *op. cit.*, *Statistical Abstract of U.S.*, 1968.

64. The low cost of transport of liquid and gaseous fuels as compared with coal has been a major factor in the decline of coal. Natural gas, the use of which has grown so spectacularly in recent decades and is now the primary source of household fuel, was regarded as a nuisance and largely wasted until the development of transportation techniques which made it possible to transport long distances from oil fields. The technological breakthroughs which made this possible were high pressure pipes, improved welding methods which made leak-proof pipelines feasible, and the introduction of heavy power equipment to reduce the cost of laying pipe.

power in ways which have had very far-reaching consequences for the growth in manufacturing productivity.

The rise of electricity began in the last decade of the nineteenth century but commenced its rapid growth only after the steam turbine had been brought to a level of efficiency which created thermal power stations and the highly centralized generation of electric power. It was this development which was mainly responsible for the decline in the coal-using steam engine which had come to dominate the provision of power to industry by the beginning of the twentieth century. The minimum size of the steam engine had always obstructed its availability to small plants and thus limited the more thorough diffusion of power, and it was also highly inefficient in those frequent situations where it had to be operated to supply small quantities of power. Moreover, the steam engine required clumsy techniques of belting and shafting for the transmission of power within the plant which were not only highly wasteful in their energy losses but also severely constrained the organization and flow of work, which had to be grouped, according to power requirements, near the power source.

The advent of "fractionalized" power which was made possible by electricity and the electric motor meant that power could now be made available in very small, less costly units and in a form which did not require the generation of excess capacity in order to provide small or intermittent "doses" of power. In addition to its direct energy-saving and capital-saving effects (not the least of which was in floor space) however, the new flexibility made possible a wholesale reorganization of work arrangements and, in this respect, made a major contribution to mass production techniques. "Shortly after steam power began to yield to electricity, installation of electric motors called attention to the obvious restraints placed upon efficiency by the steam engine. Its systems, practices, and factory organization became almost visibly redundant. Thus, as 'unit drive' electric power grew in plant after plant, thoroughgoing reorganization of factory layout and design took place. Machines and tools could now be put anywhere efficiency dictated, not where belts and shafts could most easily reach them."[65]

The speed with which electricity was adopted may be readily indicated. Electric motors accounted for less than 5 percent of total installed horsepower in American manufacturing in 1899. The growth in the first years of the twentieth century was such that by 1909 their share of manufacturing horsepower was 25 percent. Ten years later the share rose to 55 percent and by 1929 electric motors completely dominated the manufacturing sector by providing over 80 percent of total installed horsepower.[66] The sharp rise in productivity in the American economy, in the years after World War·I, doubtless owed a great deal, both directly and indirectly, to the electrification of manufacturing.

If it is true that American industry rests firmly—or, according to some harbingers of mineral supply exhaustion, precariously

---

65. Richard B. Du Boff, "The Introduction of Electric Power in American Manufacturing," *Economic History Review*, December 1967, p. 513. Du Boff also reports that the proportion of manufacturing establishments using power equipment grew as follows:

1899 –	64.0%
1909 –	68.7
1919 –	81.1
1929 –	91.8
1939 –	97.5

Ibid., p. 515. Although the diffusion percentages would have risen in the absence of electricity, it is obvious that the many advantages and cost economies of this new form of power were responsible for a large part of the growth.

66. Landsberg and Schurr, *op. cit.*, pp. 52–53.

—upon the conversion of mineral fuels into energy,[67] it is equally true that technological innovation is also improving the efficiency with which these mineral sources are utilized. During the twentieth century there has been a continuous series of technical improvements in the efficiency of centralized thermal power plants, the cumulative effects of which have been enormous improvements in fuel efficiency. Much of this improvement has involved the exploitation of seemingly inexhaustible economies of large-scale production but, in addition, a stream of minor improvements in plant design, a shift to higher pressures and temperatures and numerous other small improvements have sharply raised the output of energy derived from a physical unit of input. The magnitude of this improvement is evident in the fact that whereas it required nearly seven pounds of coal to generate a kilowatt-hour of electricity in 1900, the same amount of electricity could be generated by less than nine-tenths of a pound of coal in the 1960s.[68] Even this figure, however, understates the full improvement in the utilization of energy sources. "During the 50-year period 1907–1957 reduction of the total energy required or lost in coal mining, in moving the coal from mine to point of utilization, in converting to electric energy, in delivering the electric energy to consumers, and in converting electric energy to end uses have increased by well over 10 times the energy needs supplied by a ton of coal as a natural resource."[69]

67. The relative insignificance of hydropower sources is clearly attested to in Table 12. Hydropower has never been responsible for as much as 5% of aggregate energy consumption. What is perhaps even more surprising is that it was only as recently as during the years of the Second World War that hydropower exceeded fuel wood as a source of energy.

68. Landsberg and Schurr, *op. cit.*, pp. 60–61.

69. *Historical Statistics of the United States, op. cit.*, p. 501. The sustained improvements in energy production with conventional fuels are one of the

These magnitudes in fuel economy are worth dwelling on, not only because of the obvious quantitative significance of improvements in fuel economy, but because of the light they shed upon the nature of technological change itself. In thinking about technological change, most attention is accorded the dramatic innovations which constitute sharp departures from earlier techniques. Much less attention is accorded the small, frequently anonymous improvements in design, the substitution of slightly improved materials or the achievement of better tolerances, the minor adjustments and modifications in practice which are as frequent as they are unspectacular. The cumulative impact of these small improvements, however, can be enormous, and any perspective on technological change which fails to recognize this is necessarily distorted and incomplete. The same huge cumulative effect of a large number of small changes is particularly evident also in the iron and steel industry. Here gradual increases in size of blast furnaces and modifications in their design, the introduction of more effective auxiliary equipment for materials handling and other purposes, and continual improvement in control of combustion, temperature, and fuel utilization generally have brought major long-

reasons that nuclear power continues to have only very limited commercial application. Although nuclear fuel does not yet constitute a major energy source in the United States, it is likely that its eventual introduction will be heavily influenced by its exceedingly low transportation cost. "Even with current technology under which only a small fraction of nuclear fuel is utilized, shipping nuclear fuel probably runs no more than one-tenth the cost of shipping an equivalent heat value by the cheapest traditional energy transportation—the oil tanker. Transmission of electricity, even at highest currently feasible voltage, costs approximately 100 times what it costs to ship the same amount of energy in the form of nuclear fuel. In the long run these differences are likely to introduce substantial changes into national patterns of energy production and transportation." Landsberg and Schurr, *op. cit.*, p. 23.

term increases in the productivity of resources employed in this industry.

Finally, it is important to emphasize the extent to which future economic growth is likely to be shaped by trends in energy cost. Cheap energy, if it can be made available, may be expected to simplify a wide range of economic problems which might otherwise become increasingly intractable. This is because the cost of fuel is a major item in fuel-intensive productive processes where natural resource limitations pose problems of growing severity. Thus, food production in the future will be immeasurably eased by cheap power, with which fresh water can be made readily available for irrigation through desalination, and nitrate fertilizers provided in abundance. Similarly, cheap fuel, as mentioned earlier, will open up enormous quantities of low grade mineral deposits, not presently usable, for commercial exploitation.[70]

THE LOOSENING OF SUPPLY SIDE CONSTRAINTS

Something which is obvious from the foregoing account of technological change in American economic growth is its extreme unevenness. Technological change has never visited all sectors of the economy in a uniform, lock-step fashion. Each sector of the economy has experienced great variations, over time, in the rate of inventive activity, in the speed of diffusion of new techniques and in the nature and specific form which

70. The long-run significance of low-cost energy has been forcefully argued by Dr. Alvin Weinberg, Research Director and Director of the Oak Ridge National Laboratory, who has aptly described energy as "The Ultimate Raw Material." See, for example, chap. 1 in his book, *Reflections on Big Science* (Cambridge, Mass.: The M.I.T. Press, 1967).

these new techniques have taken.[71] Indeed, a large part of this chapter has been directly concerned with understanding these developments in terms of the economic forces which generated them and determined their shapes, as well as with their economic consequences. It seems appropriate, in closing, to emphasize the formative role played by technological forces themselves in determining the pace and direction of technological advance.

One useful way of looking at economic growth is as a progressive relaxation of two sets of supply side constraints. One set, as we have seen, is imposed by limitations in the stock of knowledge and is relaxed as this knowledge frontier is shifted outward. Thus, hybrid corn required a sophisticated knowledge of genetic processes, and synthetic materials required an advanced understanding of molecular theory. *Within* these limits, however, there is a second set of constraints imposed by the extent to which techniques that are possible with a given state of knowledge are actually realized. Thus, as we have seen, much of the innovation in nineteenth-century mechanization involved an increasing mastery of metal-working techniques, but these techniques, in turn, were available with no significant growth in the stock of basic knowledge. Most of what was accomplished in nineteenth-century mechanization involved increasing skills in the precision working of metals and the development of techniques which required imagination and mechanical ingenuity, but no fundamental breakthroughs in basic knowledge. This was true not only of manufacturing but of agriculture as well, where technical change drew heavily

71. The variations in the rate of inventive activity among industries are greater than the variations in productivity growth. This is not surprising, in view of the various mechanisms whereby improvements which originate at one point in the economy are transmitted to other sectors.

upon the mechanical skills and techniques which had been developed in the manufacturing sector.

The direction in which this expansion of knowledge is likely to go in the future is difficult to predict for many reasons. In some measure this obviously depends, as will be emphasized in the next chapter, upon allocation decisions as to the kinds of research activities which deserve to be supported. But, in addition, it depends also upon the fact that the realm of the unknown is not uniformly resistant to human probings. Some aspects of the natural world are simply more complex than others and therefore inherently more difficult to unravel. The chemical structure of Vitamin B_{12} is much more complex than Vitamin B_1 or Vitamin C and therefore took longer to synthesize and place in commercial production. Although it had long been obvious that there were enormous potential economic benefits to be reaped throughout the animal and vegetable worlds from a greater knowledge of organic chemistry, such knowledge persistently lagged behind the growing knowledge of inorganic chemistry. Even after it had become apparent that all organic substances were composed of a small number of elements—mainly carbon, hydrogen, oxygen, and nitrogen— science remained baffled at the mysteries of the organic world. Progress in organic chemistry, we now know, lagged far behind inorganic chemistry because of a basic datum of the natural world: the far greater size and complexity of organic molecules. Similarly, amorphous materials, as a group, are much more complicated in their atomic structure than crystalline solids and therefore involve a greater research effort to understand. It appears, more generally, that we may be moving up a scale of increasing complexity in the knowledge base underlying economic activity—from the mechanical to the electrical and electronic, chemical, biological, etc.[72]

It should be obvious that it is not possible to draw a sharp distinction between the two sets of supply side constraints. In a certain sense, after all, it is possible to attribute *all* constraints on what is attainable at any moment in time to limitations of knowledge. But what is more important for present purposes is not so much strict clarity between the two categories of constraints as the recognition that there are wide variations in the degree of difficulty and complexity of problems with which we are confronted and that this degree of difficulty plays an important role in determining both the timing and the direction of inventive activity. Historical instances abound of cases where innovations were conceptualized but not realized because they were beyond the technical capacity of the day. DaVinci's notebooks are full of sketches of novel machinery which could not be realized with the primitive metal-working techniques of his time. Breechloading cannon had been made as early as the sixteenth century, but could not be used until precision in metal-working made it possible to produce an airtight breech and properly-fitting case (or, in the case of firearms, cartridge).

---

72. Friedrich Engels made an analogous argument in his *Dialectics of Nature*. On the lag of agricultural behind industrial innovation, Parker makes the following interesting observation: "This technological 'lag' of agriculture behind industry is a central fact in the world's economic history and merits an analysis of its sources, extent, and consequences. I can only suggest here a succession of technological achievements in which, as in the array of mechanical inventions for harvesting, the easiest problems were solved first. The life processes, in which agriculture deals, were more deeply hidden than the mechanical processes of manufacture, and required the formation of intellectual capital at a deeper level—the invention of such machine tools as statistics and a science of biochemistry—to bring them under any appreciable degree of control." W. Parker, "Sources of Agricultural Productivity in the Nineteenth Century," *Journal of Farm Economics*, December 1967, p. 1464. See also the same author's "Economic Development in Historical Perspective," *Economic Development and Cultural Change*, October 1961, pp. 1–7.

Christopher Polhem, a Swede, devised many techniques for the application of machinery to the quantity production of metal and metal products, but could not successfully implement his conceptions with the power sources and clumsy wooden machinery of the first half of the eighteenth century.[73] The Frenchman LeBlanc who, Thomas Jefferson reported, was making muskets on an interchangeable parts basis in the 1780s, seems to have experienced a similar fate, although facts concerning his life and activities are limited.

In the development of machinery to perform specific functions, the differences in the inherent degree of difficulty at the technological level are an important factor influencing the timing of inventions. In the textile industry the mechanization of cotton preceded the mechanization of wool partly because the differences in the nature of the raw materials made cotton much more amenable to mechanized processes than wool. Although innumerable attempts to mechanize the picking of cotton go back to the 1820s (as the patent records will testify), a successful cotton picker was developed by International Harvester only in the 1920s and introduced during the 1940s during a period of rapidly rising wages. A mechanical cotton picker had to imitate (or substitute for) the complex actions of human fingers; whereas a mechanical grain reaper, which imitated the much simpler sweep of the human arm, was successfully developed in the 1830s. Similar considerations explain why a corn picker took so much longer to develop than a cultivator.[74] One

73. Usher, *op. cit.*, pp. 376–378.
74. Obviously this is not intended to suggest that technical complexity is the entire story, but merely that it is important. Wheat, for example, had a peculiarly urgent seasonal peak labor requirement which was not true of cotton or corn, and in this sense the demand for the reaper may be said to have been more urgent.

of the reasons for the persistence of coal in the face of strong competition from other fuels has been the inability thus far, in spite of prolonged exploration, to develop a satisfactory technique for producing iron without the use of high-grade coal. Although other fuels have been readily substituted for coal in various uses, the substitution in metallurgical processes poses special difficulties.

Finally, we may close this chapter with brief mention of the computer, not only because it has already been responsible for so many changes in the organization and conduct of economic activity, but also because its history nicely illustrates both sorts of supply side constraints which have been mentioned as influencing the timing and direction of inventive activity. Charles Babbage had already conceived of the main features of the modern computer over a hundred years ago, and had incorporated these features in his "analytical engine," a project for which he received a large subsidy from the British government. Babbage's failure to complete this ingenious scheme was due to the inability of the technology of his day to deliver the components and methods which were indispensable to the machine's success.[75] Now that the electronic computer is a reality, a century later, its speed and capacity in data processing have made possible new directions of scientific inquiry which are, in turn, advancing scientific knowledge in many directions which would not have been possible without its assistance. Thus, not only does science contribute to the advance of technology but improvements in technology are, in turn, critical to the further advance of science. It is curious how little attention the latter

75. S. H. Hollingdale and G. C. Tootill, *Electronic Computers* (London: Pelican, 1965), p. 46 and chaps. 2 and 3.

relationship has received. Although the contributions of science to technology have been extensively studied and catalogued, the immensely significant contributions of advances in technique to the development of science have been badly neglected.

CHAPTER VI

Technology and Social Options

Our examination of the changing economic role of knowledge in the last chapter raises a wide range of questions. Many of these questions, which are highly relevant to an understanding of economic change as well as to the formulation of effective economic and social policies, center upon the changing conditions of knowledge production and the manner in which this knowledge is utilized. The knowledge industry, it appears, is not entirely like other industries. It has some special characteristics which need to be understood especially since technological change and social change generally are now more closely linked to the output of this industry.

From an economic point of view, perhaps the most striking peculiarity of knowledge production is that it is not possible to establish the nature of its production function. We can never predict the output which will be generated by a given volume of inputs. By its very nature knowledge production deals with forays into the unknown. It involves the commitment of resources to an exploratory process the outcome of which may be a large number of dead ends rather than the hoped-for discovery of knowledge or techniques possessing profitable economic applications. The development of hybrid corn, discussed ear-

172

lier, was a spectacular example of a successful search, but not necessarily a representative example.[1] This high degree of risk, which is inseparable from the activity involved, imparts a strong downward bias to the willingness of private firms in a free enterprise society to undertake investments in such activities.[2] Since it is impossible for risk averters to shift these risks completely, society as a whole will underinvest in such activities.

Moreover, our patent laws notwithstanding, the output of the knowledge industry is privately appropriable only to a very limited degree, especially where basic scientific research is in-

---

1. Schultz has collected together the results of several studies—American, Mexican, and Japanese—which suggest that the social returns to organized agricultural research have, indeed, been very high. See Theodore W. Schultz, *Economic Growth and Agriculture* (New York: McGraw-Hill, 1968), p. 85.

The history of the development of hybrid corn does illustrate forcefully one interesting consequence of research activity which follows from the high degree of uncertainty which is inevitably involved. That is, the examination of a range of phenomena from a purely scientific perspective, with no immediate concern for practical results, may lead to the disclosure of economically valuable knowledge which may readily be missed by people with a more applied orientation who are looking for the immediate solution to practical problems. As Nelson has observed: "During the latter half of the nineteenth century several attempts were made to improve corn yields. Many of the researchers directed their attention, at one time or another, to the inbreeding of corn to obtain a predictable and profitable strain. But as corn plants were inbred, though they tended to breed true, they also tended to deteriorate in yield and in quality. For this reason, applied researchers attempting to improve corn dropped this seemingly unpromising approach. But George Harrison Shull, a geneticist working with corn plants and interested in pure breeds not for their economic value but for experiments in genetics, produced several corn strains that bred true and then crossed these strains. His project was motivated by a desire to further the science of genetics, but a result was high-yield, predictable hybrid corn." R. Nelson, "The Simple Economics of Basic Scientific Research," *Journal of Political Economy*, June 1959, pp. 301–302.

2. See Kenneth Arrow, "Economic Welfare and the Allocation of Resources for Invention," in *The Rate and Direction of Inventive Activity, op. cit.* Arrow refers to the ". . . fundamental paradox in the determination of demand for information; its value for the purchaser is not known until he has the information, but then he has in effect acquired it without cost" (p. 615).

volved. Therefore discrepancies between the private and social rates of return on such expenditures are not only numerous but often very large as well. That is to say, research expenditures which may generate great benefits to society as a whole may also generate very small benefits—or perhaps no benefits at all —to the private firm making such expenditures. However, it would involve an intolerable—perhaps even an inconceivable —set of restrictions upon human behavior to coerce all members of society into treating knowledge as a fully appropriable good so that such benefits could be "privatized."

But, more important, it would be undesirable as a matter of social and economic policy to allow such knowledge to be privately appropriated. Any restrictions which are placed upon the use of an *existing* stock of knowledge constitute a departure from optimal resource use. For knowledge is, in this respect, a public good possessing the distinctive characteristic that more for me does not mean less for you, a good which is not *used up* in the process of being *utilized*. Any legal restrictions on utilization therefore deprive some members of society of a cost-less benefit, and in this sense constitute a violation of the conditions of "Pareto optimality." From this point of view, the limited effectiveness of our patent laws in capturing the economic value of research activity sponsored by private firms may be a blessing rather than a misfortune. But this brings us directly to the confrontation which poses a major dilemma for social policy: In order to make knowledge production privately profitable, restrictions must be placed upon the *use* of knowledge; but any restrictions upon the use of existing knowledge lead to under-utilization and therefore violate the conditions of static efficiency.[3]

3. See Paul Samuelson, "The Pure Theory of Public Expenditure," *Review of Economics and Statistics,* November 1954, pp. 387–389; and Richard Nelson,

It seems apparent that the market mechanism by its own operation does not provide a sufficient incentive for the allocation of resources to knowledge production. The growing utilization of knowledge in economic activity, then, is likely to increase the discrepancy between the private rate of return and the social rate of return upon investment in knowledge.[4]

Of course this limited effectiveness of market forces in achieving a sufficient allocation of resources to knowledge production has been recognized, at least implicitly, for a long time. Although the late nineteenth and early twentieth centuries have witnessed the emergence of numerous private industrial research laboratories, some of which have been spectacularly successful (Du Pont, Bell Telephone, Eastman Kodak, General Electric) the financing of research activity, particularly basic research, has been increasingly accepted as a responsibility of public agencies.[5] Not surprisingly, the first important commit-

---

"The Simple Economics of Basic Scientific Research," *Journal of Political Economy*, June 1959, pp. 297–306.

4. The divergence between private and social rates of return, however, is not a sufficient condition for public investment. As Griliches points out in the conclusion of his hybrid corn study: "We must ask not only whether social returns are higher than private—this is also true of many private investments —but also whether the private rate of return is too low, relative to returns on alternative private investments, to induce the *right* amount of investment at the *right* time. The social returns from nylon were probably many times higher than DuPont profits, but the latter were high enough to induce the development of nylon without a public subsidy, although, perhaps, not soon enough. To establish a case for public investment one must show that, in an area where social returns are high, private returns, because of the nature of the invention or of the relevant institutions, are not high enough relative to other private alternatives. This was undoubtedly true of hybrid corn, and it is probably true of many other areas of agricultural research and basic research in general. But it is not universally true. Hence a high social rate of return is not an unequivocal signal for public investment." Griliches, "Research Costs and Social Returns," *op. cit.*, pp. 430–431.

5. A useful description of the role of the federal government before the Second World War may be found in A. Hunter Dupree, *Science in the Federal*

ment of government resources to research was in agriculture. In this sector the land grant colleges and the agricultural experiment stations now have a history of research and assistance in the diffusion of new techniques extending back over a century.[6]

In 1940 total R and D[7] expenditures in the United States,

Government (Cambridge, Mass.: Belknap Press of Harvard University Press, 1957).

6. See Alfred C. True, *A History of Agricultural Experimentation and Research in the United States, 1607–1925,* U.S.D.A. Misc. Publication No. 251, Washington, D.C., 1937; and *State Agricultural Experiment Stations,* U.S.D.A. Misc. Publications No. 904, Washington, D.C., GPO, 1962. See also the excellent and judicious survey by Vernon Ruttan, "Research on the Economics of Technological Change in American Agriculture," *Journal of Farm Economics,* November 1960, pp. 735–754.

7. The National Science Foundation has characterized the relevant terms in the following ways:

"Basic Research is concerned with exploration of the unknown. It is primarily motivated by the desire to pursue knowledge for its own sake. As such, it is free from the need to meet immediate objectives, but is undertaken to increase the understanding of natural laws. . . .

"Applied Research is directed to finding means by which a recognized need may be met. It draws upon the existing knowledge created by basic research and in its own turn creates additional knowledge. It differs from basic research in that it is pointed toward practical applications rather than toward investigation for its own sake. . . .

"Development is the systematic use of knowledge and understanding gained from research and directed to the production of useful materials, devices, systems and methods; such work includes the design, testing and improvement of prototypes and processes. Development is directed to generally predictable and very specific ends. . . ." National Science Foundation, *Federal Funds for Research, Development and Other Scientific Activities,* Fiscal Years 1967, 1968 and 1969, pp. 10, 15 and 20.

Thus, R and D expenditures include a diverse range of activities. Although they are often used as a measure of the volume of inputs into inventive activity, they possess many limitations for this purpose. The figures exclude much inventive activity, such as the work of individual and independent inventors. They include, under basic research, many inquiries which may be only remotely connected, if at all, with invention. Furthermore, most of what falls under the rubric of development—far and away the largest component of R and D—can hardly be regarded as inventive activity, inasmuch as it presupposes the prior *existence* of an invention which has to be modified, tested or redesigned before it can be placed on the production line. For further discussion see Simon

most of which was financed by private industry, was less than $600,000,000 and amounted to about six-tenths of 1 percent of GNP. During the war years the federal commitment of resources rose sharply and continued their growth in the late 1940s. By the early 1950s total R and D expenditures had risen to well over one percent of GNP and continued to rise, more rapidly in the post-sputnik years, until they amounted to fully three percent of GNP by the mid-sixties. As will be apparent from Table 13, almost two-thirds of all R and D expenditures in recent years has been financed by the federal government.

Such highly aggregated figures, however, fail to reveal some very significant facts about R and D spending, and Tables 14, 15, and 16 therefore provide important details about the sources and the disposition of R and D funds. To begin with, only a small percentage of total R and D expenditures was devoted to basic research—less than 15 percent in the late 1960s. Applied research accounted for slightly over 20 percent. The lion's share—about two-thirds—was devoted to development. In addition, private profitmaking organizations make only a trivial contribution to the support of basic research, most of which, although it is financed by the federal government, is actually performed at colleges and universities. In the second half of the 1960s, less than 7 percent of the total R and D expenditures of private firms was devoted to basic research (and the proportion was declining), about a quarter was devoted to applied research (and the proportion was also declining), and about 70 percent was devoted to development (and the proportion was rising). Private firms, in fact, no longer provide as much

Kuznets, "Inventive Activity: Problems of Definition and Measurement," and Jacob Schmookler, "Some Difficulties in Measuring Inventive Activity," in *The Rate and Direction of Inventive Activity, op. cit.*, pp. 19–51.

Table 13

Sources of Funds, by Sector, Used for Research and Development,
1953–70
(Millions of Dollars)

Year	Total	Federal Government	Industry	Universities and Colleges	Other Nonprofit Institutions
1953	5,207	2,759	2,239	151	58
1954	5,738	3,138	2,367	167	66
1955	6,279	3,509	2,513	185	72
1956	8,483	4,859	3,336	204	84
1957	9,912	6,119	3,460	230	103
1958	10,870	6,791	3,700	257	122
1959	12,540	8,059	4,057	290	134
1960	13,730	8,752	4,508	328	142
1961	14,552	9,264	4,749	371	168
1962	15,665	9,926	5,114	424	201
1963	17,371	11,219	5,449	485	218
1964	19,215	12,543	5,884	555	233
1965	20,449	13,025	6,541	615	268
1966	22,285	13,986	7,318	673	308
1967	23,680	14,451	8,145	753	331
1968 (prel.)	25,330	15,005	9,125	840	360
1969 (est.)	26,250	14,855	10,130	885	380
1970 (est.)	27,250	15,000	10,895	950	405

Source: National Science Foundation, *National Patterns of Research and Development Resources, 1953–70.*

Table 14

Sources of Funds, by Sector, Used for Basic Research, 1953–70
(Millions of Dollars)

Year	Total	Federal Government	Industry	Universities and Colleges	Other Nonprofit Institutions
1953	489	234	148	73	34
1954	548	265	161	85	37
1955	608	286	183	99	40
1956	747	345	239	116	47
1957	857	408	256	136	57
1958	973	460	282	159	72
1959	1,155	609	280	185	81
1960	1,326	693	331	215	87
1961	1,543	841	350	250	102
1962	1,886	1,091	382	293	120
1963	2,196	1,310	414	343	129
1964	2,560	1,593	425	402	140
1965	2,858	1,815	449	445	149
1966	3,135	1,988	496	494	157
1967	3,422	2,196	503	551	172
1968 (prel.)	3,730	2,405	525	615	185
1969 (est.)	3,730	2,345	545	645	195
1970 (est.)	3,935	2,445	585	700	205

Source: National Science Foundation, *National Patterns of Research and Development Resources, 1953–70.*

Table 15

Sources of Funds, by Sector, Used for Applied Research, 1953–70
(Millions of Dollars)

Year	Total	Federal Government	Industry	Universities and Colleges	Other Nonprofit Institutions
1953	1,317	770	455	73	19
1954	1,430	822	512	76	20
1955	1,525	842	583	79	21
1956	1,938	1,012	820	81	25
1957	2,429	1,292	1,020	85	32
1958	2,757	1,468	1,166	88	35
1959	2,965	1,624	1,208	95	38
1960	3,093	1,725	1,228	102	38
1961	3,156	1,804	1,197	110	45
1962	3,775	2,127	1,473	118	57
1963	3,881	2,205	1,487	128	61
1964	4,300	2,498	1,598	139	65
1965	4,556	2,659	1,658	155	84
1966	4,823	2,725	1,845	161	92
1967	5,093	2,851	1,960	182	100
1968 (prel.)	5,495	2,935	2,247	205	108
1969 (est.)	5,655	2,910	2,412	220	113
1970 (est.)	5,915	3,035	2,532	225	123

Source: National Science Foundation, *National Patterns of Research and Development Resources, 1953–70.*

Table 16

Sources of Funds, by Sector, Used for Development, 1953–70
(Millions of Dollars)

Year	Total	Federal Government	Industry	Universities and Colleges	Other Nonprofit Institutions
1953	3,401	1,755	1,636	5	5
1954	3,760	2,051	1,694	6	9
1955	4,146	2,381	1,747	7	11
1956	5,798	3,502	2,277	7	12
1957	6,626	4,419	2,184	9	14
1958	7,140	4,863	2,252	10	15
1959	8,420	5,826	2,569	10	15
1960	9,311	6,334	2,949	11	17
1961	9,853	6,619	3,202	11	21
1962	10,004	6,708	3,259	13	24
1963	11,294	7,704	3,548	14	28
1964	12,355	8,452	3,861	14	28
1965	13,035	8,551	4,434	15	35
1966	14,327	9,273	4,977	18	59
1967	15,165	9,404	5,682	20	59
1968 (prel.)	16,105	9,665	6,353	20	67
1969 (est.)	16,865	9,600	7,173	20	72
1970 (est.)	17,400	9,520	7,778	25	77

Source: National Science Foundation, *National Patterns of Research and Development Resources, 1953–70.*

financial support for basic research as do the universities. Furthermore, an examination of the composition of the federal government's R and D budget (which had ceased to grow at the end of the 1960s, and approximately two-thirds of which was devoted to development) would show that it has been overwhelmingly dominated by three agencies: DOD, NASA, and AEC. Indeed, these three agencies accounted for almost 90 percent of all federal R and D funds. The largest single claimant on the remaining 10 percent or so has been HEW, followed by NSF and the Departments of Agriculture and the Interior. Finally, there is also a high degree of industrial concentration of the federal and private funds which are allocated to R and D. Over 80 percent of all R and D performance is located in just five industries: aircraft and missiles, electric equipment and communication, chemicals, motor vehicles, and machinery. In fact, the first two of these five industries alone have been accounting for nearly 60 percent of the total.

Taking an overall view, it is clear that R and D spending in recent years is overwhelmingly dominated by the needs of the defense establishment, that the basic research component is very small, and that the bulk of the non-defense component is directed toward rather modest objectives, among which such items as the annual design changes of consumer durables loom very large. As one group of authors has recently commented:

Outside defense and space related R&D . . . and possibly some segments of the civil electronics and chemical industries, the bulk of corporate R&D is modest design improvement work not reaching very far—the type of work that results in yearly changes in automobile design, gradual improvements in refrigerators and vacuum cleaners, and steady improvements in the automaticity, speed, and capacity of machine tools, rather than radically new products.[8]

8. Nelson, Peck and Kalachek, *Technology, Economic Growth and Public Policy, op. cit.*, p. 54. See also D. Hamberg, "Invention in the Industrial Re-

The cumulative effects of some of these changes certainly make important contributions to the growing productivity of the economy. Much private development expenditure, however, is directed toward forms of product differentiation and techniques of consumer appeal which can hardly be regarded as possessing a high social priority—a new shade of lipstick, another synthetic detergent, yet one more filtered cigarette. Indeed, to a substantial portion of the population, the end-product of these activities is both socially wasteful and meretricious.

This growth in the public support of knowledge production, especially at the level of basic scientific research, where the private incentives are weakest, poses important questions of public policy. To a considerable degree, it is obvious that such research has become socialized, and that both the size and the direction of research efforts are increasingly the product of allocative decisions made within the public sphere. As Price has aptly expressed it, the government has "learned to socialize without assuming ownership."⁹ Much of the technological change in the past quarter century has been the result of intensive public efforts undertaken in the pursuit of goals formulated

search Laboratory," *Journal of Political Economy,* April 1963, pp. 95–115. Hamberg argues that the research laboratories of the large industrial corporations are minor sources of major inventions, although they are major sources of minor inventions ("improvements"). He concludes: "Yet without any careful consideration, the laboratories of the large industrial corporations have been receiving all the accolades and most of the support. Although it appears that the bulk of major inventions originate outside these laboratories, particularly in the work of independent inventors and small- and medium-size firms, these sources have been relatively neglected and their potential contributions virtually ignored—at least in our formal policies. It seems clear that future efforts to foster technological progress must cease this neglect and develop ways of supporting these wellsprings of fundamental advances in the arts." *Ibid.,* p. 115.

9. Don K. Price, *The Scientific Estate* (Cambridge, Mass.: Harvard University Press, 1965), p. 43.

in relation to the needs of national security—jet propulsion, numerical control, computer technology and electronics more generally, and atomic energy.[10] However, it will not do to extrapolate past experience uncritically into the future. The spillover from military research into civilian uses has been real enough, but one cannot simply assume that equally important spillovers will continue. Indeed, there seem to be compelling reasons to believe that they will not. Military technology is now so highly complex and specialized that it is probably several "generations" ahead of the civilian sector and possible peaceful applications. The spillovers from mission-oriented projects of the kind sponsored by DOD and NASA are not likely to be very substantial, and spokesmen for these agencies have vastly—and somewhat disingenuously—exaggerated their significance in recent years. There may be a compelling case to be made for the development of new military hardware—more effective weapons delivery systems or more sophisticated (and incredibly costly) anti-missile techniques. That case, however, is essentially

10. The manner in which ordinary contractual relationships have been transformed in the government's present arrangements with industrial suppliers for the military—particularly in industries such as aircraft and electronics—is suggested in the following observations: "In dollar volume, the biggest contracts are between the military services and industrial corporations. Though most of this money goes for procurement, much of it goes for research and development, and for the systems analysis and the direction and supervision of subcontractors that in a simpler age would have been done by the technical services of the Army and Navy. And even in the business of procurement, the contractual relation is not the traditional market affair: the contract is not let on competitive bids, the product cannot be specified, the price is not fixed, the government supplies much of the plant and capital, and the government may determine or approve the letting of subcontracts, the salaries of key executives, and a host of other managerial matters. A sizable proportion of the government's (and nation's) business is done this way; each of five industrial corporations spends more than a billion dollars a year from federal taxes—which is more than any one of five of the executive departments." Price, op. cit., pp. 37–38.

military and strategic, and not economic or social.

The conclusion is inescapable that the manner in which we allocate our research resources makes a great deal of difference to the kinds of techniques we eventually develop and the kinds of problems we succeed in solving. The point—not very startling—seems worth emphasizing in view of a widespread tendency to discuss research and development in global terms and to ignore questions concerning its composition. Uncertainties, spillovers, and serendipity notwithstanding, it remains true that the most effective way of solving specific problems in the civilian sector is to allocate research expenditures directly to those problems. If a substantial proportion of the resources presently committed to military R and D were transferred to civilian R and D purposes, all evidence suggests that the result would be an accelerated rate of technological change and productivity growth.[11] The opportunity costs to society of military research, in short, are extremely high, because such research is absorbing precisely those scarce human resources which might otherwise be employed in a forthright assault upon social problems of a high degree of urgency.

Our growing sense of frustration in some areas of our national

11. Two studies provide empirical confirmation for this proposition. Minasian found that, within a particular industry, there was a significant correlation (.70) between expenditures upon R and D and an individual firm's productivity growth. J. Minasian, "The Economics of Research and Development," in *The Rate and Direction of Inventive Activity, op. cit.* Terleckyj, on the other hand, found a significant correlation (.62) between the amount of R and D spending (and employment of scientists and engineers) in an industry and its productivity growth. That there was a substantial unexplained variance is not surprising in view of the frequency with which industries benefit from technological changes which originated elsewhere. Nestor E. Terleckyj, *Sources of Productivity Change. A Pilot Study Based on the Experience of American Manufacturing Industries, 1899–1953,* unpublished doctoral dissertation, Columbia University, 1959, as reported in John W. Kendrick, *Productivity Trends in the United States* (Princeton, N.J.: Princeton University Press, 1961), pp. 177–187.

life surely reflects a collective failure to allocate research resources to areas which have been relatively neglected—education, medical care,[12] air and water pollution, urban housing, public transportation systems and the whole range of urban services. It is obviously becoming a matter of growing importance that we develop institutional mechanisms for formulating and achieving goals in areas of our national life, other than defense, where the market mechanism has proven to be an unsatisfactory instrument. This is likely to involve an even greater reliance upon the not-for-profit organizations, which perform much of the research financed by governmental agencies. Such organizations are and doubtless will continue to play an increasingly important role in the production and distribution of knowledge. But, more generally, there is an urgent need for developing new forms of collaboration between the public and private sectors which will direct our technological potential more forcefully toward the solution of nonmilitary problems.[13]

12. Medical *research* has been, on the whole, well financed. There may, however, be a very high social payoff to research directed toward providing improved systems for the *delivery* of medical care. Moreover, it is at least arguable that medical research has been too well financed—that growing research opportunities in the medical profession have drawn an excessive number of doctors away from the more routine but essential provision of medical care within the framework of existing knowledge and techniques.

13. Even within the private sector of the economy the impact of a growing reliance upon knowledge production is not well understood, although it seems apparent that firms—or at least departments of firms—which are strongly oriented toward research are significantly different in their organizational features from firms conducting their business with relatively stable technologies. Research departments of large firms, for example, seem to possess a much higher degree of informality of structure and interpersonal relationships, and certainly operate toward a more distant time horizon than do other departments—production, sales, etc. It may well be that variation in organizational forms is more closely related than we had previously been aware, not so much to the *kind* of technology employed, but to the frequency with which it changes due to successive increments to the underlying knowledge base. A dimension which needs to be explored then, in addition to the kinds of technology, is the stability

The increasing socialization of knowledge production also raises serious questions concerning the adequacy of the legal and institutional framework of business enterprise. Consider our patent system. This system embodies the notion that some forms of knowledge may be treated as private property. The assumption is that the knowledge was privately produced in the first place in response to a reward system which permitted such private ownership and exploitation. Historically, this system goes back to Article 1, Section 8 of the Constitution, which states that "The Congress shall have Power . . . to promote the Progress of Science and useful Art, by securing for limited Times to Authors and Inventors the exclusive Right to their respective Writings and Discoveries." The relevance of such a privatized, individualistic conception is very much open to question in a society where the bulk of the resources devoted to knowledge production are financed by the public sector and where the isolated, single investigator, although by no means gone, is being replaced by a collective enterprise among cooperating specialists. Whether these individuals work in a private firm, government agency, or university laboratory, they are very likely to be salaried employees whose incentive structures only remotely resemble the ones assumed in the patent law.

Clearly the rewards held out by the patent system exert an influence upon the allocation of resources to inventive activity, although it is much more likely now than it was in the early nineteenth century to influence a business firm's decisions with respect to the *hiring* of technically-skilled personnel rather than an inventive individual's decision concerning the alloca-

or instability of the unit being administered as a result of its dependence upon changing inputs of knowledge. Needless to say, such variations carry with them important implications for the effective discharge of managerial responsibilities.

tion of his own time and energies among alternative uses.[14] The changed circumstances of knowledge production raise the question, however, whether society is making a reasonable "deal" in permitting restrictions upon the diffusion and exploitation of valuable knowledge in exchange for the incentive which it provides for the allocation of talented resources into potentially patentable research activities. The whole impact of the patent system in fact needs to be subjected to a cost-benefit analysis. Although the magnitudes would be exceedingly difficult to quantify, the form of the investigation can at least be made conceptually clear. Since there have always existed incentives to invent even in the absence of a patent system, we would have to establish the size of the *increment* to total inventive activity resulting from the patent laws. The benefits of the patent system are the increase in output which society owes to that class of inventions which would not have been made at all in the absence of that system, plus the increase in output owing to the earlier introduction of inventions which would have come anyway, but at a later date. The costs of the system are the *restrictions* in output for which the patent laws are responsible by allowing all holders of patented inventions[15] to exclude others from their use during the period of patent protection. It is an inescapable aspect of this system that, to the extent that it offers protection to the holder of a patent, it does so by slowing down the diffusion of inventions. Thus, the patent system increases output in some ways (benefits) and restricts it in others (costs). It is obviously impossible to establish the precise magnitude of

14. Further, the present patent law reinforces the bias toward applied technology and product development, where it offers protection, and away from more basic research, where it does not.

15. Including those inventions which would have been made even without a patent system, but which fall equally under its umbrella of protection.

these two variables. Nevertheless, the retention of the system presupposes that the benefits exceed the costs, and this presupposition is, under present circumstances, certainly far from obvious.[16]

Additional questions about the propriety of the legal framework, within which the modern business enterprise operates, are forcefully posed by the growing problems of environmental pollution. For present purposes we may regard property rights as the set of socially-sanctioned rules which regulate the freedom to enjoy benefits and to impose costs.[17] Such rules have worked reasonably well in regulating wide areas of human behavior and interaction. It is becoming increasingly apparent, however, that these rules, which have been developed with respect to the use and disposition of privately held assets, lead to serious misuse of property which is not privately owned—i.e., common property resources. The extent of the pollution of our two most important common property resources, air and water, is a direct consequence of the fact that our present system of property rights imposes few restrictions upon the freedom of individuals to use common property resources in this way. It

16. For an excellent historical and analytical examination of the patent system, upon which this last paragraph has drawn, see Fritz Machlup, *An Economic Review of the Patent System*, Study of the Subcommittee on Patents, Trademarks, and Copyrights, 85th Congress, 2d Session, Washington, 1958. A highly critical treatment of our present patent laws is presented in Seymour Melman, *The Impact of the Patent System on Research*, Study of the Subcommittee on Patents, Trademarks, and Copyrights, 85th Congress, 2d Session, Washington, 1958.

17. "Harming a competitor by producing superior products may be permitted, while shooting him may not. A man may be permitted to benefit himself by shooting an intruder but be prohibited from selling below a price floor. It is clear, then, that property rights specify how persons may be benefited and harmed, and, therefore, who must pay whom to modify the actions taken by persons." Harold Demsetz, "Toward a Theory of Property Rights," *American Economic Review, Papers and Proceedings*, May 1967, p. 347.

should constitute no surprise that facilities for the disposal of waste will be intensively utilized when they are "free" to the individual user while alternative techniques of disposal have substantial price tags attached to them. Such unrestricted access to common property did not matter much when population size was much smaller and widely dispersed in a rural context. However, a combination of larger and more densely concentrated populations exploiting a much more powerful technology is now producing environmental damage which is increasingly regarded as intolerable. Our common property air and water resources are, quite simply, overloaded as a result of unrestricted rights of access.[18]

Clearly the way to motivate people to behave differently is to assert the community interest in these common property resources: to introduce modifications in our present system of property rights which will compel individuals to internalize some portion of the costs which they now impose upon their

---

18. "Consider . . . the earthy and undramatic problems of waste disposal in urban centers and of pollution in general. These clearly require policy decisions at the societal level. But it was not always so. Families in sparsely settled regions were once free to dispose of their waste on the basis of self-interest; they did not adversely affect the environment of others. The habit so formed persisted when cities came into being. Progressive cities then proscribed use of the streets as sewers, and substituted direct discharge into rivers, lakes, and oceans. In terms of local interest this is reasonable—sewage treatment is expensive. But it is becoming anachronistic for large communities to determine their methods of disposal independently. The problem has been greatly augmented by the growth of industrialization. The wastes of modern industry have reached huge volume. In terms of individual interest, industrial firms—paper mills, chemical plants, refineries, and so on—find economy in downstream disposal of untreated waste and heat, but this reduces and often destroys the value of the streams for individual use, recreation, and other purposes. In terms of their interest, it is equally reasonable for great metropolitan centers to claim pre-emptive rights to regional waters for waste disposal, as when Chicago reduces water levels in the Great Lakes to flush its sewage down the Mississippi River." Barnett and Morse, *Scarcity and Growth, op. cit.,* pp. 254–255.

external environment. This can be achieved in a variety of ways: regulation, subsidy, or by a system of charges for the right to pollute the common property resource in question. Whichever devices are adopted, they must involve a recognition of a community interest in certain portions of the natural environment[19] and the legitimacy of a new set of property rights regulating the access of individuals to this environment.[20]

There are a variety of different approaches through which financial or legal constraints upon business firms may be manipulated in order to reduce the deleterious side-effects of technology. These approaches, however, share one common feature: they are costly. Any serious discussion of the ecological consequences of modern industrial techniques must confront this issue directly.

It should no longer be necessary to rehearse the numerous ways in which the present functioning of modern technology is inflicting damage—in some cases irreversible—upon our natu-

19. And, it should hardly be necessary to add, the man-made environment as well. In 1969, for example, New York City streets were littered with no less than 57,000 abondoned cars. The declining price of scrap metal has rendered it uneconomic for the owner of an "expired" automobile to arrange for it to be hauled off the city streets. Although it is a violation of a city ordinance to abandon a car in this manner, enforcement has been rendered very costly because of the difficulty of establishing the owner's identity after he has removed the license plate and filed off the engine number. For a useful discussion of some of the legal, political, and technical problems in the attempt to control urban pollution, see Merril Eisenbud, "Environmental Protection in the City of New York," *Science*, 13 November 1970, pp. 705–712.

20. The policy alternatives for dealing with the problem of pollution of common property resources are treated in an absorbing little book: J. H. Dales, *Pollution, Property and Prices* (Toronto: University of Toronto Press, 1968). Dales favors a system of fees for the right to discharge waste materials into common property resources. See chap. 6: "Pollution Rights." Of course, no scheme requires the *total* elimination of pollution unless society were to decide that it was prepared to pay the enormous costs which such elimination would involve.

ral environment. This has been extensively catalogued and graphically depicted elsewhere. Indeed, every ecologist seems to have his own special chamber of horrors on industrial man's (or would-be-industrial man's) apparently unlimited capacity for fouling his own nest. The evidence is indeed overwhelming that we have, in the past few decades, introduced powerful new agents into our environment—insecticides, herbicides, fertilizers, radiation, industrial waste—with an astonishing indifference to their possible ecological consequences. There can hardly be serious disagreement on the need to award a much higher priority to the improvement of our understanding of these interactions and to monitoring and anticipating future deteriorations. There is no excuse for allowing actions to be undertaken, which may have significant ecological consequences, without the best possible information or estimate of the likely nature and scope of these consequences.

Such assessments, however, should not be expected to make the decision-making procedure an easy one, but merely a better-informed one. That is to say, they will clarify and perhaps in some cases quantify the alternatives with which society is confronted. For the simplistic, ultra-conservationist view, which assumes that the mere identification of an activity as a source of pollution is a sufficient reason for terminating the activity, is not, and never has been, a viable one. We must face up to the fact that it is quite impossible to utilize any sophisticated technology—or, for that matter, many primitive ones—without engaging in numerous actions which alter some important dimension of the environment.[21] Indeed, in view of the

21. As Lynn White, Jr. has recently pointed out: "Ever since man became a numerous species he has affected his environment notably. The hypothesis that his firedrive method of hunting created the world's great grasslands and helped to exterminate the monster mammals of the Pleistocene from much of the globe is plausible, if not proved. For 6 millennia at least, the banks of the lower

tendency to wax nostalgic over a rural and bucolic past, it is worth remembering that one of the most drastic of all ecological distrubances, with respect to its impact on wildlife, was the conversion of forest and plain to cropland.[22]

The important point to be made here, however, is not only that ecological disturbances are unavoidable but that the more objectionable forms of these disturbances are usually the outcome of a decision to adopt the cheapest technique available for a given productive process. This is most obviously the case where the offending substances are waste materials which are indiscriminately discharged into the atmosphere or the nearest body of water. That is to say, pollution is in large measure the product of deliberate decisions to minimize the direct costs of production on the part of a business firm or a public utility or a municipal government. We could eliminate much of it if we decided—or if we allowed ourselves to be persuaded—that we were prepared to give up some portion of our material output in exchange for a more attractive and liveable natural environment. Everyone wants unpolluted rivers and streams just as everyone laments the death of Lake Erie.[23] But not everyone

Nile have been a human artifact rather than the swampy African jungle which nature, apart from man, would have made it. The Aswan Dam, flooding 5000 square miles, is only the latest stage in a long process. . . ." Lynn White, Jr., "The Historical Roots of Our Ecologic Crisis," *Science*, 10 March 1967, p. 1203.

22. For a detailed treatment of the effects of westward expansion upon wildlife in America, see Peter Mathiessen, *Wildlife in America* (New York: Viking Press, 1959).

23. As well as the impending damage to the unique ecology of Lake Baikal. The recent heated controversy in the Soviet Union over the pollution of Lake Baikal by the effluvia of a new paper mill sharply underlines the fact that certain painful social choices are independent of economic systems, in spite of the efforts of several decades of Marxist critics to pin the tail of pollution and environmental destruction firmly upon a capitalist donkey. Indeed, all evidence suggests that the Soviet Union is moving into the same range of environmental problems as those with which we are currently contending. Her lag is primarily a function of lower income levels and population densities. One wonders, for

is prepared to pay his share of the huge costs of alternative methods for the disposal of industrial and municipal waste. Such unwillingness, surely, is the critical element. Merely to deplore the deterioration of our natural environment is to be on the side of the angels—that is, it does not genuinely confront the real issues. After all, if such destruction were merely wanton, if it could be terminated at no cost whatever, it would presumably be done immediately. The relevant question is how much we are prepared to pay to purify the Potomac or the Hudson or the Charles. How much urban renewal, medical research, foreign aid, and vocational rehabilitation are we prepared to forgo so that our rivers may run pure once again? Such questions, such scrutiny of our individual and collective values are, I submit, the ones to which we should now be addressing ourselves.

The fact is that techniques are presently available for achieving a high degree of purity of our water systems. One rough estimate places the annual cost of returning effluents to water courses in a state of "pristine purity" at around $20,000,000,-000.[24] When confronted with an annual bill of this magnitude, it is not at all obvious that pure water constitutes a "Best Buy" rating, and society may well decide to tolerate a considerable amount of pollution. Twenty billion dollars could purchase a great deal of food or provide a very large amount of medical care or vocational training. Some portion of it, if intelligently spent, might even help to bring America's high infant mortality rate down to something like respectable western European levels. Happily, the decisions confronting us here are not of the

example, how successful the Soviet regime will be in suppressing the privately owned automobile as the demand for them increases with rising incomes.

24. Allen V. Kneese, "Research Goals and Progress Toward Them," in Henry Jarrett (ed.), *Environmental Quality in a Growing Economy* (Baltimore: Resources for the Future, 1966), p. 71.

all-or-none variety. There exist a gradation of degrees of water purity, greater than the very low state which we presently tolerate, which are available at progressively higher cost, all the way to the upper bound estimate for pristine purity.

We can, moreover, with our *present* technology, also substantially reduce the amount of air pollution emitted by the electric utilities in big cities either by removing the offending substances prior to combustion, or by burning fuels which are more expensive but contain smaller amounts of these substances. In this respect fuel oil is preferable to bituminous coal and natural gas is preferable to both. A large part of our present air pollution, in other words, is not an inevitable product of our present technology but rather the product of decisions to utilize low cost fuel supplies.[25]

A related complication, in addition to the high absolute cost of reducing pollution, is the likely distributional consequences of measures to reduce pollution. A rise in electricity bills due to the employment of higher cost fuels is likely to weigh most heavily upon low income receivers; and the compulsory installation of an expensive automobile exhaust filter will push very few Cadillacs off our highways but will almost certainly result in the disappearance of numerous battered old jalopies which

25. "In most large cities . . . the electric utilities consume up to half of all fuel burned. Most utilities have made reasonable efforts to reduce the emission of soot and fly ash; virtually all new power plants, and many old ones, are now equipped with devices capable of removing a large fraction of such emissions. Utilities, however, are still under pressure, both from the public and from supervising agencies, to use the cheapest fuels available. This means that in New York and other eastern-seaboard cities the utilities burn large volumes of residual fuel oil imported from abroad, which happens to contain between 2.5 and 3 percent of sulfur, compared with only about 1.7 percent for domestic fuel oil. When the oil is burned, sulfur dioxide is released. Recent studies show that the level of sulfur dioxide in New York City air is almost twice that found in other large cities." Abel Wolman, "The Metabolism of Cities," *Scientific American*, September 1965, pp. 187–188.

often constitute the only practical form of transport available to the rural and urban poor.[26] Specific measures to reduce pollution may turn out to be in direct conflict with the goal of reducing poverty.

The painfulness of the choices with which we are confronted may be forcefully seen in a different context. The public has been made increasingly familiar in the past few years with some of the deplorable side-effects of insecticides, herbicides, and commercial fertilizer. Yet these inputs, as we have seen, have played a crucial role in the growth of farm output in the United States in the past thirty years. The use of such inputs was instrumental in the production of the large wheat surpluses which have recently been shipped to India during years of crop failure in that country. Without question, the willingness to employ these new chemical inputs in agriculture has had as a direct consequence, on at least one occasion, the avoidance of mass starvation in India. When this evidence is placed in the balance, the moral self-righteousness of some of the unqualified opponents of the use of such inputs may be seen in a distinctly different light. What, after all, is the final value judgment placed upon the use of a chemical agent which damages birds and wildlife at home, and at the same time provides life-saving food for the Indian subcontinent?

The relevant issues may, of course, be more complicated than the last example suggests, but this is a matter for careful investigation and demonstration and not bald assertions. If, for example, the use of such chemicals had a long-run cumulative effect in reducing soil fertility, say through ecological disturbances or through upsetting bacteriological activities, the situation may

26. Older cars are also, of course, usually the main offenders against clean air.

then become an unstable one. That is to say, higher productivity today is being purchased at the price of lower productivity at some future date. Although the use of these agents may still be justified, the circumstances which would provide such justification would clearly have to be more compelling when the process involved was unstable or irreversible. It is an urgent matter that we vastly improve our understanding of the impact of such actions upon the long-term productivity of our resource environment. Clearly there is sufficient work in hand here for whole generations of ecologically-trained specialists. Does a particular practice on some particular scale constitute a nuisance to the present generation—an offense to the olfactory senses perhaps—but nothing more? Does it, by its impact upon the food chain, threaten the prospects for a particular species which we are anxious to preserve—say, hawks or eagles? Or does it threaten some wholly intolerable transformation of the environment? There are mechanisms in Nature through which she occasionally wreaks a fearful revenge (Nature's backlash) upon the human enterprise, and we have, without question, enormously increased our capacity to evoke such reactions. Unwise irrigation practices in ancient Mesopotamia eventually ruined her topsoil (and thereby destroyed her civilization) through the resulting excess salinity. Overgrazing of arid grasslands in the Middle East and elsewhere has converted untold millions of acres of productive soil into useless desert. The upsetting of the delicate ecological balance in swidden farming has resulted in apparently irreversible transformations in Southeast Asia—transformations leading to a replacement of forest by *imperata* savannah grass which has turned parts of that region into an ecological system sometimes described as a green desert. Finally, closer to home, agricultural malpractices created for the United States the awesome "Dust Bowl" of the 1930s. Clearly there are ecological disturbances of varying degrees of severity, and they should not be treated as a homogeneous collection of offensive phenomena. Some of them we may decide we can—and perhaps should—safely ignore. Others we can ignore only at our great peril. It seems therefore to be extremely important that we learn to discriminate among the many ecological interactions which are going on around us. Not all of them are equally urgent in their demands upon our attention—although it is of course true that in the present state of our ignorance we often simply do not know how urgent some of them are or may become. It is more than a little disconcerting, for example, that the experts have been continuously revising in a downward direction their estimates of radiation dosages to which human beings can be "safely" exposed.

In some measure, technology itself may be invoked to reduce the painfulness of the choices which confront us. It is possible to put our sophisticated technology to work at the task of reducing the destructiveness of some of the obnoxious side effects of modern technology, or even to providing new uses for waste materials. It is really an old story that new technologies create problems which require offsetting or remedial actions within the technological sphere, just as, throughout history, new offensive weapons have generated responses in the form of improvements in the technology of defense. Similarly, many of the gloomy, ecologically-based forecasts will doubtless turn out to have been excessively pessimistic because they underestimated our capacity for undertaking corrective action using the tools of modern science and technology.[27] It seems to be unfortunately

27. Just as technological events have repeatedly falsified conservationist predictions of the impending exhaustion of essential natural resource inputs. A major thrust of modern materials science has been to broaden the range of substitutes, especially by learning to exploit abundant materials in place of

true, however, that governments are crisis-oriented and fail to initiate remedial action until a problem appears to assume crisis proportions.[28] Nevertheless, in some limited areas progress is

scarce ones. This has been of particular significance with respect to the utilization of low-concentrate resources, a development which (so long as cheap power is available) holds open an almost limitless potential for the future. For a perceptive treatment of this subject see Barnett and Morse, *Scarcity and Growth, op. cit.* To the conservationist's preoccupation with the shrinking heritage of natural resources and the need to preserve them for future generations, Barnett and Morse retort: "In the United States . . . the economic magnitude of the estate each generation passes on—the income per capita the next generation enjoys—has been approximately double that which it received, over the period for which data exist. Resource reservation to protect the interest of future generations is therefore unnecessary. There is no need for a future-oriented ethical principle to replace or supplement the economic calculations that lead modern man to accumulate primarily for the benefit of those now living. The reason, of course, is that the legacy of economically valuable assets which each generation passes on consists only in part of the natural environment. The more important components of the inheritance are knowledge, technology, capital instruments, economic institutions. These, far more than natural resources, are the determinants of real income per capita." *Ibid.*, pp. 247–248.

28. More generally, the forces influencing a society's decision to allocate resources to the solution of particular problems is a subject which needs to be more throughly explored. National defense considerations aside, society's perception of an unfulfilled need is often shaped by a particular event—a natural disaster, a serious accident, or a national sense of inadequacy and urgency resulting from a dramatic accomplishment elsewhere. The massive growth in American support to certain areas of science, technology, and education following the launching of the Soviet sputnik is merely one of the most recent spectacular cases in point. At a more local and individual level, events such as boiler explosions, the collapse of bridges or the sinking of vessels on the high seas have served as powerful focusing devices. Sensational disasters such as fires at sea were almost always followed by a rush of patent applications for devices which purported to prevent their recurrence. Nobel's invention of dynamite (which, it should be remembered, is a comparatively safe explosive) owed much to the distinctly unfortunate tendency of his nitroglycerin shipments to explode in transit aboard railroad trains or, in some spectacular instances, in mid-ocean. The bursting of a hydraulic cylinder due to the enormous pressure to which it was subjected during the raising of the Britannia Tubular Bridge across the Menai Straits in the late 1840s led directly to systematic experimentation and, eventually, important advances in knowledge concerning the crystallography of metals. For further discussion see Nathan Rosenberg, "The Direction of

already being made. Many agricultural chemicals of recent development decompose more rapidly than did their predecessors into harmless substances. Modern detergents are incapable of rising up into billowing mountains of foam as they once did under an earlier formula. But even the tamer detergent formula took some fifteen years of diligent and expensive chemical research to develop.[29]

It simply will not do, then, to state, as do some of the apocalyptic writers on the subject, that many of our modern ills are readily traceable to "Modern Technology" and leave the matter at that. This is, at best, simply a half-truth. The other half of the truth is that these ills are a product of human choices. We have *chosen* not to reduce the unpleasant side-effects of our technology in at least two important ways. First, we have failed to devote more of our resources to seeking out new techniques for reducing these side-effects just as we have chosen to allocate the great bulk of our research efforts to military purposes, to the neglect of the civilian sector; and, second, within the spectrum of alternatives offered by the present state of our technology, we often select alternatives which are less costly in terms of money outlays but which generate higher levels of pollution— as in the case of our choice of fuels. From this perspective,

Technological Change: Inducement Mechanisms and Focussing Devices," *Economic Development and Cultural Change,* October 1969, pp. 1–24; Jacob Schmookler, "Catastrophe and Utilitarianism in the Development of Basic Science," in Richard Tybout (ed.), *Economics of Research and Development* (Columbus: Ohio State University Press, 1965), pp. 19–33; John G. Burke, "Bursting Boilers and the Federal Power," *Technology and Culture,* Winter, 1966, pp. 1–23; "Report of the Commissioners appointed to inquire into the Application of Iron to Railway Structures," *Parliamentary Papers,* 1849, vol. 29.

29. Furthermore, although detergents are now "bio-degradable," their high phosphate content continues to act as a fertilizing agent encouraging the growth of algae. In this respect detergents remain an important contributor to algae pollution in rivers and lakes.

environmental damage is simply the result of decisions to adopt less costly methods of production. We are free, of course, to make such choices, through our public as well as through our private institutions. However, if we do, we have no right to complain about their consequences.

Index